11. **Financial report.**
    a) Recognize the treasurer to presen report.
    b) Recognize members for question; motion to adopt the report as presented.

12. **Committee Reports.**
    a) Recognize members for the presentation of any committee reports.
    b) Recognize members for motions pertaining to committee reports.

13. **Announce any unfinished business, and entertain motions relative thereto.**

14. **Elections.**
    a) Announce vacancies in any offices for which elections must be held.
    b) Recognize nominations from the nominating committee and from the floor.
    c) Recognize for a motion that the nominations be closed.
    d) Announce that the vote is on the election of nominees; count the vote and announce the results of the election.

15. **Announce that new business is now in order.**

16. **Recognize members to offer motions or propose resolutions.**
    a) Recognize members to debate or amend the main motion.
    b) After each vote announce whether the proposition has carried or failed.

17. **At the conclusion of all business, recognize members to make announcements.**

18. **Recognize for a motion to adjourn.**

DESCHLER'S RULES OF ORDER

DESCHLER'S RULES

OF ORDER

by Lewis Deschler

PRENTICE-HALL, INC., Englewood Cliffs, New Jersey

DESCHLER'S RULES OF ORDER
by Lewis Deschler

Printed in the United States of America
Prentice-Hall International, Inc., London
Prentice-Hall of Australia, Pty.Ltd., Sydney
Prentice-Hall of Canada, Ltd., Toronto
Prentice-Hall of India Private Ltd.,
New Delhi
Prentice-Hall of Japan, Inc., Tokyo
10 9 8 7 6 5 4 3 2 1

Library of Congress Cataloging in
Publication Data
Deschler, Lewis.
    Deschler's Rules of order.
    Includes index.
    1. Parliamentary practice. 2. United
States. Congress. House—Rules and
practice. I. Title. II. Title: Rules of order.
JF515.D45   060.4'2   75-40226
ISBN 0-13-219543-7

PREFACE

The membership organizations that hold meetings every day probably number in the tens of thousands. Whether business or fraternal, religious or social, governmental or civic, labor or educational, these groups have a common need: to govern themselves democratically and fairly and at the same time to execute the will of the majority. Parliamentary law provides the framework and procedures by which these objectives can be met.

The forerunner of what we know today as parliamentary law probably precedes recorded history, being rooted no doubt in early tribal customs. We do know that over a thousand years ago King Edgar, one of the first rulers of a united England, developed elementary rules and regulations enabling individuals with conflicting interests to gather and discuss their grievances in a fair and orderly manner. Some three centuries later these rules were adopted and expanded by the English Parliament—hence the present name, "parliamentary law." The term "parliament" itself is derived from the French word *parler*, meaning "to speak." Of similar derivation is the word "parley," which usually signifies a conference or meeting between persons of opposing factions.

Parliamentary law has been in widespread use throughout the world for the past seven centuries. But never in our history has the need for parliamentary law been more self-evident. Parliamentary law makes it possible for an assembly to govern itself at all times in an orderly way, whether that be at the international, national, state, or local level.

There is probably no subject more universally misunderstood than parliamentary law. I have received countless requests from organizations seeking my assistance in resolving some parliamentary problem with which they were confronted. Long-distance telephone calls from a presiding officer of a state legislature concerning some parliamentary crisis have not been uncommon. In the past, time permitting, I have always tried to be helpful. I can now refer persons making inquiry to this book, for in it I have attempted to provide simplified parliamentary procedures that can be understood by anyone, whether lawyer or layman.

Simply stated, parliamentary law is a tool that enables an assembly to deliberate upon a problem with full and free debate and to take definite action. It protects two fundamental rights: the right of an individual or the minority to be heard and to have a vote, and the right of the majority to act despite efforts by a minority to frustrate or thwart the will of the majority.

This book is an outgrowth of my experience as parliamentarian of the U.S. House of Representatives for nearly fifty years. Since its inception, the House has formulated rules for its procedure. Today they are perhaps the most finely adjusted and balanced rules of any legislative or parliamentary body in the world, having been hammered out over a period spanning nearly two centuries. Under them a majority may work its will at all times in the face of the most determined and vigorous opposition of a minority.

In preparing this book, I have taken the approach that the House parliamentary system is readily adaptable to any membership organization that needs some form of parliamentary procedure. I have simplified and generalized that system in such a way that it will be applicable to any membership organization, large or small, legislative or nonlegislative.

My second objective in preparing this book was to ensure that the system set forth is one based on the law. I have therefore cited the more important court cases throughout and have included references to the House Rules and precedents, which have been frequently construed by the U.S. Supreme Court. As an additional feature, I have included a set of model rules, which may be adopted by any membership organization by so providing in their bylaws.

The precedents cited in this work are the rulings of the presiding officers of the House; these precedents are to the Rules of the House what the decisions of the courts are to the statutes. They are found in *Hinds' Precedents of the House of Representatives* (Washington, D.C., 1907) and *Cannon's Precedents of the House of Representatives* (Washington, D.C., 1936), cited herein simply as, for example, "1 HP Sec. 123" or "6 CP Sec. 456."

It is my view that the House parliamentary procedure, as construed by the distinguished lawyers and jurists who have presided over it and as interpreted by federal courts, is the most authoritative to be found in the Western world. Clearly, it is a system upon which a membership organization can safely rely in resolving procedural or parliamentary problems or in seeking judicial enforcement of its rights.

The House rules are the most comprehensive and efficient of any legislative body. I recall a conversation with a member of a parliamentary organization who criticized the motion for the previous question as used in the House as "archaic." When I replied that the motion, though probably several hundred years old, was effective, widely recognized, and well understood, he asked, "A motion to close debate would be just as good wouldn't it?" "Of course not," I answered, and explained that a motion to close debate does nothing except terminate debate on the main proposition, whereas a motion for the previous question not only ends debate but prevents the offering of amendments or other motions of lesser precedence.

Any membership organization wishing to locate and more thoroughly review the Hosue Rules or the decisions of presiding officers concerning those rules, as found in Hinds' or Cannon's precedents, will find these publications available in various public law libraries or in any one of the depository libraries, which include the highest state appellate court libraries, state libraries, libraries of independent government agencies, and military libraries. Information concerning the location of the depository libraries (of which there are more than one thousand) may be obtained by writing a member of Congress. The publications referred to may be purchased from the U.S. Government Printing Office (Superintendent of Documents, Washington, D.C. 20402).

Readers who wish to look up a case cited in this work may do so by consulting the *National Reporter System*, published by the West Publishing Company and available in nearly all law libraries. It consists of two main divisions: (1) opinions of the state appellate and trial courts and (2) opinions of the federal courts.

The system of state court reporting was initiated in 1879 with the *North Western Reporter*. The state reporting units consist of seven regional reporters arranged roughly by geographical divisions—the *Atlantic Reporter, North Eastern Reporter,* etc.

These reporters currently report state appellate court decisions in full; they provide the complete text of each decision and often include headnotes as well as digests of the briefs of counsel.

Coverage of federal cases is found in the *Supreme Court Reporter*, which reports in full every decision of the Supreme Court of the United States beginning with the October term of 1882; the *Federal Reporter*, which includes the decisions of the U.S. Court of Appeals; the *Federal Supplement*, which reports decisions of the United States district courts since 1932.

Case reports are commonly cited by names of the parties, volume and page of the report series, and date of decision. Often, a case will be cited in such a way as to show that it appears in two separate series of reports—a state report and a unit of the *National Reporting System*. Thus, where a case is cited as "*Wynn* v. *Sullivan*, 294 Mass. 562, 3 N.E. 2d 235 (1936)," it means that the case appears in Volume 294 of the *Massachusetts Reports*, at page

562, and also in Volume 3 of the *North Eastern Reporter*, Second Series, at page 235.

The abbreviations of the regional reports are:

Atlantic Reporter..............."Atl." or "A." and "A. 2d"
North Eastern Reporter ....."N.E." and "N.E. 2d"
North Western Reporter ...."N.W." and "N.W. 2d"
Pacific Reporter ...."Pac." or "P." and "P. 2d"
South Eastern Reporter ....."S.E." and "S.E. 2d"
South Western Reporter ...."S.W." and "S.W. 2d"
Southern Reporter............"So." and "So. 2d"

Lewis Deschler
Bethesda, Maryland

CONTENTS

—1—

HISTORICAL BACKGROUND: DEFINITIONS AND DISTINCTIONS

Sec. 1. In General; Purpose of Parliamentary Rules

Whenever people assemble together to achieve their objectives collectively and democratically, they follow certain procedures known as "rules of order." These rules are based on principles of parliamentary law.

"Parliamentary law" is a term used to designate the body of rules and precedents regulating the modes of procedures and course of debate in legislative and other deliberative assemblies. By extension, the term has been applied to the rules governing the procedure and conduct of membership organization meetings generally, whether of business groups, associations, or fraternal societies and clubs.[1]

Adherence to rules of order makes for a healthy, well-organized, and efficient meeting. Failure to observe these rules can lead to dissension, misunderstanding, inefficiency, and loss of those individual rights associated with a democracy. As Thomas Jefferson wrote, "whether these [rules] be in all cases the most rational or not is really not of so great importance. It is much more material that there should be a rule to go by than what that rule is; that there be a uniformity of proceeding in business not subject to the caprice of the Speaker or captiousness of the members."[2]

---

[1]*Funk and Wagnalls New Encyclopedia.*

[2]Lewis Deschler, *House Rules and Manual* (Washington, D.C.: U.S. Government Printing Office, 1973), Sec. 285. Hereinafter cited as House Rules.

Rules of order are designed to enable people who meet together to solve common problems or attain mutual objectives to govern themselves in an orderly fashion and with fairness to all concerned. These rules, like other laws governing social behavior, have evolved over years of experience in democratic institutions of all kinds. These rules have been applied, modified, and extended in much the same way as the common law has evolved in the United States. Parliamentary law, like the common law, came to the United States from England, where it had evolved over a period of centuries.

Parliamentary law is designed to aid in determining the wishes of the majority and to execute those wishes but at the same time to protect the right of the minority to be heard.

A person joining a democratic organization as a member knows that in such a group the majority rules, and that in joining such a group he is agreeing to abide by the will of the majority.

"The voice of the majority decides," wrote Jefferson, "for the *lex majoris partis* is the law of all councils, elections, &c., where not otherwise expressly provided." (House Rules, Sec. 508.)

At the same time, the minority has the right to take part in discussions and to oppose actions contemplated by the majority. Parliamentary law protects these rights as jealously as it does the rights of the majority.

Sec. 2. Kinds of Membership Organizations

Americans are joiners. Membership organizations have proliferated in this country to a degree perhaps greater than any other Western nation. Alexis de Tocqueville, reporting on the tendency of Americans to organize, wrote in his *Democracy in America* (1835):

> Americans of all ages, all conditions, and all dispositions constantly form associations. They have not only commercial and manufacturing [associations], in which all take part, but associations of thousands of other kinds, religious, moral, serious, futile, general or restricted, enormous or diminutive. The Americans make associations to give entertainments, to found seminaries, to build inns, to construct churches, to diffuse books, to send missionaries to antipodes; in this manner they found hospitals, prisons, and schools.

Membership organizations do indeed take many different forms and engage in a wide variety of activities. Some are primarily service organizations, such as the American Bar Association and the American Medical Association; each supplies information to members in the form of newsletters and magazines and in response to specific requests.

Other types of organizations are primarily "product" oriented and engage in marketing and supply activities of various kinds. They can no longer be divided easily into distinct categories, however, as more and more of them expand their services and activities each year. This trend toward diversification has continued upward with each decade and is even more marked among the larger membership organizations.

Because of this great diversity in form and scope of interests, it is difficult to define the elements that are common to all organizations of this nature. It is safe to say, however, that all of them (or nearly all of them) have four separate and distinct parts: (1) members, (2) a board of directors, (3) elected officers, and (4) staff or hired management. It is also true that the basic principle common to all of them is that fundamental ownership and control is in the hands of the members.

The terms "association" and "society" are probably the terms most frequently used by membership organizations in describing themselves. However, there are countless other terms used to designate them, including "conference," "forum," "convention," "board," "club," "congress," "chamber," "federation," "committee," "academy," "foundation," and "institute." These terms have no special legal or parliamentary significance in themselves, but are important in communicating something as to the nature of the organization to the public.

Sec. 3. Federated Membership Organizations

A "federated" membership organization is one that is comprised, in whole or in part, of a number of local, state, or regional membership organizations. Usually, the local or regional organization holds membership in the national or parent body, but often the relationship is more of an affiliation rather than actual membership.

Sometimes a federated organization will consist of both state or local organizations *and* individuals or firms. For example, the American Trial Lawyers Association consists not only of many thousands of attorneys and law firms but also of many state trial lawyers' associations throughout the country.

A wide variety of reciprocities regarding membership is recognized between the national organization and the local or state affiliates or members. Sometimes an individual or firm must first belong to his state or regional organization before becoming eligible for membership in the national organization. In other instances, membership in a state or regional organization will automatically make the individual or firm a member of the national or parent body. Finally, it is occasionally required that the individual or firm join both the national and the local organizations in order to become eligible for membership in either.

The voting rights of a national federative organization may be vested in (1) individuals or firm members holding direct memberships, (2) the state, local, or regional membership organizations, or (3) both.

There are many advantages of organizing on a "federated" basis:

1. It produces better communications between the local individual member and his organizations at the national level.
2. Local participation in and action on programs of interest to the national organization can be obtained.
3. It enables the parent body to concentrate on national problems.
4. It creates a greater interest and participation on both the local and the national levels.
5. Local identity and autonomy are maintained.
6. It enables the national organization to speak with a unified voice on matters of importance.
7. It increases membership at both the national and the local levels.

There is generally no agreement between the national organization and the locals or regionals as to which will conduct specific activities; however, most national organizations have found it desirable that their individual members receive direct communications from the local or regional organizations in the federation. And in cases where the firm or individual members of the national organization do not receive direct communications from the state or locals in the federation, the national organization will often relay information to their members.

Although national or "federated" associations are not required to share dues with state or regional members, a few do in fact share dues with local affiliates. Sometimes as much as 10 to 20 percent of the amount paid to the national is sent to the state or local organizations. More frequently, the state or local organization in the federation will collect the membership dues and send the national a certain percentage or predetermined amount. The most common arrangement is for the national to collect dues solely from individual or firm members, without imposing any financial obligations on the affiliated member organizations.

Sec. 4. Local or Regional Membership Organizations

As indicated above, many state, local, or regional membership organizations hold membership in a national association that represents their field of interest or activity.

There are many advantages enjoyed by state and local organizations through a federation:

1. They can present a unified voice for their industry or field of activity at the national level.
2. It facilitates at the local level the promotion and coordination of activities and the exchange of information.
3. It allows the state and local organization to concentrate on local affairs.
4. It enables local organizations to apply expertise acquired at the national level.

Various reciprocities exist between the state or regional organizations and the parent body. Ordinarily, an individual or firm in a particular industry or field of activity need not first hold membership in the national in order to become eligible for membership in the local. However, in many instances, membership in the local will automatically make the individual or firm a member of the national or parent body.

Ordinarily, a member or group of members from the local or regional organization, with voting rights, will sit on the board of directors of the national or parent body to represent the local or state organization.

Many local or state organizations send a portion of their dues to the national or parent body. The amount sent to the parent body is either a flat rate per member or a percentage of the amount paid by the member to the state or local.

Sec. 5. Trade Associations and Professional Societies

Trade associations were among the first membership organizations to be formed in the United States. The American Bankers' Association was founded in 1876; the National Association of Cotton Manufacturers was formed in 1854.

Professional societies are among the most active and influential of American membership organizations. The American Bar Association was formed in 1878, and the predecessor of the American Institute of Certified Public Accountants was formed in the 1880s.

Scientific societies originated in Europe during the Renaissance period. One of the oldest scientific societies in this country is the American Academy of Arts and Sciences, founded in 1780. It was followed by the formation of such scientific membership organizations as the American Medical Association (1847), the American Association for the Advancement of Science (1848), and the American Society of Civil Engineers (1852). During the latter part of the nineteenth century, scientific and technical societies grew in number and membership and became increasingly significant agencies for the acquisition and diffusion of knowledge.

The major activities of trade associations and professional and business societies are centered in the field of education. These activities include the sponsorship of clinics, short courses, workshops, and institutes, as well as the preparation of workbooks for training purposes. Trade shows are also an important educational activity.

Other areas of special interest to such groups are public relations, standardization, simplification of practices, employer-employee relations, and accounting.

Another key area of interest of societies and associations lies in the field of government relations. Members are informed of governmental regulations and laws; the members, in turn, are enabled to express their views on legislative issues through the organization. The drafting of model legislation is also a significant organization activity. And many assist governmental agencies and legislative bodies by supplying facts on production, distribution, sales, etc.

The organizers of a trade association or a professional society, just as any other membership organization, should adopt bylaws and rules consistent with the foregoing activities and interests. Model bylaws and rules for such an organization are set out elsewhere in this work. (See Sec. 44.)

Sec. 6. Cooperatives

A cooperative is a membership organization of a special kind. It is a business formed by a group of people to obtain certain services for themselves more effectively or more economically than they can obtain them individually. These people both own and operate the business for their mutual benefit. By working together through the cooperative, the member-owners find that they can obtain services not available to them otherwise.

Among the many different kinds of cooperatives are farmer cooperatives, mutual fire and life insurance associations, urban or rural consumer cooperatives, electric and telephone cooperatives, wholesaling businesses owned by retailers, and the like.

The various types of cooperatives may be classified as follows:

Marketing cooperatives are those in which the major portion of their total dollar volume is derived from the sale of products for its patrons or members. Many of these also purchase supplies and perform related services for their members. Some of these are classified by the type of commodity handled.

Supply cooperatives are those in which product-supply constitutes the major part of their total annual dollar volume of business. Many such cooperatives also market products and perform related services.

Bargaining cooperatives are those engaged primarily in bargaining to obtain the most advantageous price for a certain product or line of products for its patrons or members. Some of these also process products for their members.

Service cooperatives are those engaged primarily in providing services to members, such as supplying educational or promotional services, or services pertaining to particular products, such as storage and transportation.

A *local cooperative* is essentially a local association providing cooperative services for members in a particular community or county or even several counties. Local associations may or may not be affiliated with other cooperatives.

A *regional cooperative* is one that usually serves a district comprising a number of counties, an entire state, or a number of states.

A *federated cooperative* is one that directly serves other cooperatives, primarily local member associations. Cooperatives with no individual members are classified as *federated regionals* regardless of the size of the region or area served.

Mixed-membership cooperatives are those that are not wholly federated but have both local cooperatives and individuals as members. In fact, such a cooperative may include other cooperatives, individuals, partnerships, and corporations in its membership.

It is thus clear that cooperatives perform a wide variety of functions. They may be formed to market products, for example, as in the case of farmer cooperatives. They may be formed to purchase supplies or other commodities, as in the case of food cooperatives. Or their function may be merely to provide such services as water and electricity.

A significant trend in this regard is toward multiple-service cooperatives. In some farmer cooperatives, for example, a member may process and market several products, obtain farm production supplies through it, and even secure such services as production advice, market news, and insurance.

Cooperatives vary greatly in size and in the range of services they provide. They range from small local cooperatives, with only a handful of members, to large national or regional cooperatives with hundreds of thousands of members. The large regionals may in turn be broken up into smaller local cooperatives, all of which obtain certain common services from the parent cooperative, which are in turn passed on to the individual members of the locals. Some of the large regional cooperatives have both individuals and local cooperatives as members.

In many ways, cooperatives are organized like other businesses and operate in much the same fashion. They usually incorporate under the laws of the states in which they operate or have their headquarters. They prepare bylaws and other necessary legal documents. The members elect a board of directors, which in turn hires a manager and sets policy. The manager executes the policies of the board and operates the business in such a way as to best serve the members.

Cooperatives are to be distinguished from other kinds of businesses in many important respects. First, voting control in a cooperative is based on membership and not on amount of investment, as in the case of the usual corporate structure. Ordinarily, each member of the cooperative has only one vote. Moreover, savings over the cost of doing business are distributed to member-owners in proportion to their use of its services, not in proportion to their investment. Dividends on invested capital are limited.

Another important distinction is that the operations of a cooperative are always conducted on an "at-cost" basis. Money realized from the operation of the cooperative over and above expenses belongs to those members who patronize it. Since costs cannot be estimated accurately in advance, the patrons usually pay the "going or competitive price" for goods or services purchased through the cooperative; and they generally receive an advance for products marketed by their cooperative less than the actual value of the product. Adjustments and patronage refunds are then made at the end of the year when costs are known. Such cooperatives operate at cost, not to make a profit, a distinction that is most important in determining tax advantages.

Sec. 7. Credit Unions

A credit union is a special kind of membership organization. It is a savings and lending cooperative, operated for the mutual benefit of all its members. It is member-owned and member-operated. Its primary objective is to provide an adequate and dependable source of credit for credit union members who need to borrow.

Credit unions are most numerous in urban areas but also are used in rural areas to reinforce and supplement the programs of local banks, credit associations, and other lending agencies. They provide a common meeting place for the person with money to lend and the person who needs to borrow.

The authority of a credit union is defined in its charter and bylaws, and its operations are governed by the Federal Credit Union Act (12 U.S. Code Secs. 1751 *et seq.*) and similar state credit union legislation.

The members control the operations of their credit unions. The specific requirements for membership are spelled out in credit union bylaws. Ordinarily, a member must pay an additional membership fee and buys or pledges to purchase one or more shares in the credit union.

Although local members own and operate their own local credit union, each one is usually part of a larger group of credit unions. And most belong to state credit union leagues.

The credit union members seldom participate in its day-to-day management. They elect officials who in turn choose people to carry on routine credit union business. These officials are responsible to the members.

A board of directors is elected to administer the programs of the credit union, and a credit committee is established to approve member loans.

The directors choose the executive officers from among their own group. The president, vice-president, and secretary perform the usual duties associated with those offices, whereas the treasurer usually acts as the general manager of the credit union.

The treasurer is thus the key figure in any credit union and is its principal financial officer. He is responsible for all its resources, for transactions with members, and for bookkeeping and financial reports. Of all of the credit union's officers, he is the only one who may receive a salary for his work as manager.

All credit unions are required by law to have a supervisory committee to conduct internal audits and supervise the operations of the credit union. In federally chartered credit unions, the board of directors appoints the members of this committee. State laws vary in this respect. In some states the board appoints the members, whereas in others the membership as a whole elects them.

Sec. 8. Political Action Committees; Lobbying Organizations

Membership organizations have been formed to receive political contributions from individuals and to distribute these funds to the campaigns of appropriate candidates. These organizations, known as political action committees, must receive contributions solely from individuals and not from companies or trade associations, for the latter are barred from making such contributions by federal statute. Similar restrictions apply to labor unions.

Under the controlling federal statute, it is a criminal offense for any corporation or labor organization "to make a contribution or expenditure in connection with any election" involving candidates for Congress or other federal office. This restriction applies to all incorporated membership organizations. (See 18 U.S. Code Sec. 610.)

In this connection, one should carefully distinguish between contributions for a particular candidate and contributions that are made for the political education activities of the committee. The committee may receive contributions in connection with encouraging voting, voter education, and the like. There is no legal objection to this, since these are nonpartisan activities.[3]

These statutory restrictions do not prohibit all political activity on the part of the employees of a regular membership organization, even though such activities may be directed to the support of a particular candidate. Otherwise, any political activity of any person on its payroll would render it (and its principal officers) liable, if

[3]G. D. Webster, *The Law of Associations* (Washington, D.C.: American Society of Association Executives, 1971), p. 118.

such persons devoted any appreciable time on behalf of the organization in support of, or in opposition to, any candidate for President, vice-president, senator, or representative in Congress.[4]

Care must be taken to avoid any direct or indirect involvement of any trade association or its member companies in the operation or the organization of a political action committee. However, the names of members of a political action committee, as listed on its letterhead, may include some individuals who have been or who are members of the board of directors of, for example, a trade association.[5]

A question may arise as to when activities by a membership organization become "expenditures" within the meaning of the statute. Of course, if the organization makes a specific expenditure for campaign literature on behalf of a particular candidate, the statute would apply. But an organization may, in its regularly published journals, express its views, whether critical or favorable, with respect to particular candidates. In other words, as long as the organization expresses its views with respect to a particular candidate through regular organization channels, such as monthly newsletters, periodic weekly bulletins, or the like, the money spent in this regard will not be construed as an unlawful "expenditure" within the meaning of the statute.[6]

Political action committees are required by statute to maintain in some detail records of contributions and expenditures. The treasurer of the committee must file a detailed statement with the clerk of the House of Representatives concerning certain receipts and expenditures of the committee, and naming in certain instances any donor. (See 2 U.S. Code Secs. 242-44.)

The organizers of a political action committee should adopt bylaws, consistent with the foregoing, just as any other membership organization. Model bylaws for such a committee are set out elsewhere in this work. (See Secs. 32 *et seq.*)

Lobbying

Lobbying is controlled under a statute known as the Federal Regulation of Lobbying Act. (2 U.S. Code Secs. 261-70.) This statute is designed to require public disclosure of lobbying activities. Those

[4]See *U.S.* v. *Construction and General Laborers Local Union*, 101 F. Supp. 869 (1951).

[5]See Webster, *The Law of Associations*, pp. 112, 113.

[6]See 40 NYU L. Rev. 1033.

subject to the law, including membership organizations, must register and file reports specified in the statute. The law requires the keeping of detailed accounts of contributions and receipts therefor, as well as the retention of receipted bills of expenditures. (2 U.S. Code Sec. 262.)

The scope of this statute had been limited by the Supreme Court to so-called direct lobbying; that is, lobbying that involves direct communication with Congress or its members. Not covered by the statute is "indirect" lobbying, which is the preparation and distribution of general publicity, such as pamphlets, press releases, and broadcasts.[7]

In determining whether or not an organization or individual is subject to the law's registration and reporting requirements, one must look to the language of the statute itself. This language has been interpreted by the Supreme Court in *U.S.* v. *Harriss* to mean that certain requirements must be met before the statute will apply. These prerequisites are summarized as follows:

1.   A person must have solicited, collected, or received contributions.

2.   One of the main purposes thereof must have been to influence the passage or defeat of legislation by Congress.

3.   The method of accomplishing this purpose must have been through direct communication with members of Congress.

All of these prerequisites must exist before an organization or individual will be deemed subject to the statute. If any one of them is absent, the statute does not apply.[8]

---

[7]See "Legislative Handbook for Associations," U.S. Chamber of Commerce, 1961, p. 33.

[8]*U.S.* v. *Harriss* 74 S. Ct. 808, 347 U.S. 612 (1954).

—2—

FORMING A MEMBERSHIP ORGANIZATION

Sec. 9. First Meeting of Potential Members

The idea for a membership organization usually begins in the mind of one individual, who recognizes that he has a need that is shared by others and that the need they share can be met through group action. He then discusses the matter with several friends who, in turn, realize that they have a common problem that they cannot solve individually. They may be doctors, for example, who need to keep abreast of changes in medical science; or they may be farmers who lack a market for their products; or they may be investors with a common interest who need to increase their purchasing power.

In any event, they talk their problems over informally, recognize that others may have similar needs or problems, and conclude that a membership organization might be the solution. Next, they try to discover what, in general, would be involved in starting such an organization. They seek out someone, usually a lawyer, who can advise them as to the organization-forming process.

With the help of their adviser, the leaders then get together the facts and figures they need in order to present the idea to other potential members. During this period, they usually discuss the idea informally with many others in the community, in an attempt to get some measure of the common interest.

Having discussed their problem and determined that a membership organization may be the solution, the starting group calls a general meeting of potential members. The purpose of this meeting is to determine whether there is sufficient interest in forming a membership organization to proceed further. If sufficient interest is displayed at this meeting, the next step to be taken is the ap-

13

pointment of a committee to survey the conditions under which the organization may best function.

The timing and location of the first meeting should be as convenient as possible for those who will be invited to attend. And since this meeting is not subject to the notice requirements of more formal meetings of membership organizations, invitations to the meeting may be extended by any available means—by announcements at other meetings, through newspapers, or merely by word of mouth.

The starting group should plan a definite program for this meeting and select a chairman. The chairman should be someone who can conduct a businesslike meeting. It is desirable to have an adviser, preferably someone with parliamentary experience, to be on hand at the meeting to assist the chairman.

In this first meeting, no one need commit himself to become a member, and it is not necessary to adopt policies or even to suggest guidelines for the possible conduct of the organization. However, even at this early stage, the chairman should be using parliamentary procedures to bring about orderly, democratic group action. In this way, the chairman can lead the group smoothly and efficiently to the determination of the wishes of the majority, while at the same time protecting the rights of the minority.

The first item on the meeting program should be a well-prepared factual presentation of the proposed membership organization. This may be done by having one member of the starting group discuss the common needs and problems, and for another member to summarize how the proposed membership organization might solve them. If possible, it is desirable to have a representative from some other successful organization of similar nature present to describe its various benefits and advantages.

A discussion period should follow this presentation. At this time, those at the meeting can be encouraged to express their views and ask questions, which the starting group should be prepared to answer. The chairman or his parliamentary adviser should be prepared to answer these questions.

After thorough discussion, the chairman should inquire of those present if there is sufficient interest to proceed with a more detailed study of the advantages of forming the organization. The chairman may do this simply by asking for a show of hands.

If sufficient interest is expressed, the chairman then appoints a committee, called the survey committee; this committee, with the help of a legal adviser, should be instructed to prepare a survey of all aspects of the proposed organization and to report back to the group at a later meeting. Target dates should be agreed upon for completion of the survey and for periodic reports to the group on the progress of the committee.

The chairman should exercise great care in making appointments to the survey committee. He should recognize that balance and special skills will be needed on the committee and that those appointed to it are likely to be the same persons who will later organize the membership and become the first directors of the organization.

Sec. 10. The Survey Committee

The survey committee is a committee appointed by the chairman, as noted above, at the first meeting of the potential members of the organization. Its primary functions are twofold: It must first determine whether the proposed organization is likely to be advantageous and beneficial, and, second, it must suggest a general organizational framework in which the group can achieve its objectives.

The survey committee should set forth its recommendations in a carefully prepared report. This report should contain relevant factual information, both pro and con, and it should indicate the various alternative courses of action that are available.

The subjects to be surveyed by the committee should include the facilities that might be needed, some estimate of operating costs, the size of the potential membership, the special skills that might be needed, financial requirements, and similar topics.

It will be necessary, of course, for the committee from time to time to seek out experts or specialists in such fields as finance, law, and accounting. The committee might also seek the advice of someone with experience in a similar membership organization.

In addition, there are legal and parliamentary requirements that should be taken into account at each step of the survey committee's work. Here again, expert advice from qualified individuals should be sought.

The survey committee should recognize that eventually the organization will need a full-time executive director or manager. Hence, the committee should assure itself that if the organization is formed, a good manager can be found to run it. No matter how urgently the organization may be needed, it cannot succeed unless sound management is at the helm.

The survey committee must ascertain the extent to which land, facilities, and equipment will be needed and the approximate cost thereof. The committee should consider the possibility of leasing existing facilities, as well as the possibility of building a new facility. The advice of engineers should be sought out if elaborate facilities are to be required.

The survey committee must arrive at some estimate as to the anticipated operating costs of the organization. Operating costs include such items as salary of the hired management, the cost of utilities, the taxes, and the cost of supplies. These costs should be itemized in the report that is to be made to the next meeting of the potential members.

Another problem to be considered by the survey committee is that of finance and capitalization. In other words, it must determine how much money will be needed to start the organization and how much money will be needed to maintain it for given periods of time. This in turn leads to the question of the source of capital, whether it is to be drawn from membership fees, stock issuances, or the like.

The survey committee should also investigate the various sources of long-term loans. In its report, the committee should recommend the credit source that can supply the financing most nearly suited to the needs of the organization. The main sources of such loans are banks, insurance companies, and even other or membership organizations.

The survey committee should also estimate the amount of financial reserves that the organization should build and the method of providing them. The committee should be prepared to recommend whether reserves over and above an amount considered adequate should be returned to members, in the same manner as a revolving fund. And the committee should bear in mind that in some states the amount or percent of reserves must be maintained at a specified amount by law. (See Sec. 30 *infra*.)

Other matters that the survey committee should explore include (1) whether to incorporate (see Sec. 20 *infra*), (2) the territory from which the membership is to be drawn, qualifications for membership, and membership fees, (3) the manner in which the members are to be represented on the board of directors, and (4) whether an organization agreement is to be used (see Sec. 12 *infra*).

Still other matters that should be explored by the survey committee include the name of the organization, voting procedures, and the rules for management of the organization. The survey committee should make a list of these items and their recommendations concerning each. The committee should look to its parliamentary adviser for assistance in surveying such matters.

Finally, the survey committee should estimate the cost of getting organized and set the amount each prospective member should be assessed to pay these costs. The estimates should include the cost of attorney's fees and any fee for filing articles of incorporation.

The survey committee should sum up its findings and set down its decisions and recommendations in an orderly fashion. The report should include all the relevant facts and figures collected by the committee, and it should have them on hand when it reports to the prospective members.

The survey committee report may serve as a blueprint for the organizing committee, at least to the extent that the recommendations of the survey committee have been agreed to. This means that the survey committee report should be voted upon and that voting should continue until all changes are agreed to.

Sec. 11. The Organizing Committee

The tasks of the organizing committee are as follows: (1) to sign up members, (2) to arrange for the first meeting of such members, (3) to obtain the capital or financing needed as estimated by the survey committee, (4) to draft the legal organization papers, (5) to file articles of incorporation, if necessary. The organizing committee will also wish to further investigate many of the subjects tentatively explored by the survey committee. It should bear in mind, however, that no binding agreements can be made by the organizing committee, because the organization is not yet legally in existence.

An organizing agreement, described elsewhere (Sec. 12 *infra*), may be used to sign up members. The committee may wish to enlist others to help in making a canvass of *all* prospective members in the area. If the area to be covered is large, it is desirable to assign different teams to each locality or district.

After enough members have signed up to ensure the necessary capital, the organizing committee should collect capital subscriptions from all persons who have signed an organization agreement or similar document. The funds so collected should be turned over to someone designated by the committee, who should keep a record of all such subscriptions.

The selection of a name for a membership organization is another function of the organizing committee. If incorporated, the selection of a name for the organization should comply with any corporate statutory requirements. In most states the name must not contain any term that suggests that it is organized for any purpose other than the one or more purposes contained in the articles of incorporation. In addition, the name must not be the same as, or deceptively similar to, a name already in use by another corporation existing under the laws of the state.

Under common law principles relating to unfair competition, one membership organization may enjoin another's use of an established name, even though neither conducts a trade or business.[1] Protection of an incorporated association's name or trademark is also provided by the Trade Mark Act of 1946. (15 U.S. Code Secs. 1051-1127.) In this regard, trademark infringement does not depend on a fraudulent intent, and the good faith of the infringer is no defense if the mark used is likely to result in confusion.[2]

The organizing committee may find it necessary to choose several names initially to avoid any conflict with established enterprises, submitting the names to the Secretary of State for reservation for protection. Unless the name is acceptable in all states in which the organization will operate, it may be forced, by law, to change its name.[3]

Sec. 12. The Organizing Agreement

An organizing agreement may be used by the organizing committee to determine the extent of interest in the proposed membership organization. By signing this document, the signer commits himself to belong to and patronize the proposed organization and to furnish a specified amount of initial capital, provided a certain number of other prospective members also sign up within a given time.

If the required number of members sign this agreement, the signers then meet and decide by vote whether enough signatures have been obtained to justify forming the organization.

A form for an organizing agreement is set out elsewhere in this

---

[1]*Supreme Lodge of the World* v. *Independent, Benevolent, and Protective Order of Moose*, 98 N.J. Eq. 598, 131 A. 447.

[2]*Beatrice Foods Co.* v. *Neosho Valley Coop. Creamery Ass'n*, 297 F. 2d 849.

[3]CCH *Corporation Law Guide*, Para. 210, 1969.

work. (See Secs. 34 *et seq.*) It should be borne in mind that this form, like all other legal forms of a membership organization, may have to be modified to conform to local law and should be checked by an attorney. After this has been done, and before being put to use, the form should be presented to the members of the organizing committee for their vote of approval.

Sec. 13. First Meetings of Charter Members

The charter members of the membership organization should hold their first meeting as soon as practicable after the organizing committee has concluded its work, and, if incorporated, not later than thirty days after the articles of incorporation have been filed. The main purpose of this meeting is to adopt bylaws for the organization and to conduct other organizational business.

Only those persons named in the articles of incorporation attend this first meeting as charter members to adopt the bylaws. They are deemed members for the purpose of adopting the bylaws as soon as the articles of incorporation are filed.

Further action must be taken to make members of those who have agreed to become members but who are not named in the articles of incorporation. In fact, under some statutes, the incorporators can adopt the bylaws as incorporators rather than as members.

Being not yet organized, the group will find it impractical to mail out notices of the meeting, a usual requirement for all membership organizations. Therefore, a waiver of notice of the meeting should be prepared in advance, and this should be signed by all members in attendance. A sample of such waiver of notice is set out below.

WAIVER OF NOTICE OF FIRST MEETING OF MEMBERS

We the undersigned, being all of the incorporators of [NAME OF ASSOCIATION] of [TOWN], [STATE], constituting all of the present members of such association, hereby waive notice of meeting of the members and consent to the holding of a meeting of such members at [TIME OF DAY] on [MONTH, DAY, YEAR], at [PLACE OF MEETING] in [TOWN, STATE], for the purpose of adopting bylaws for the government of the association and transacting any other business that may properly come before this meeting.

Witness our signatures, this [DAY] of [MONTH YEAR].

[SIGNATURES]

At this initial meeting, the clerk or secretary should prepare a roll of those members present and qualified to participate in conducting the business at hand. If those persons in attendance must possess certain qualifications in order to participate, a procedure should be established for checking credentials. (1 Hinds' Precedents[4] Sec. 14.) If the right of someone to participate is challenged, the chairman may direct him to stand aside temporarily. (1 HP Secs. 143-48.)

This first meeting is conducted by a temporary chairman, who begins by reporting the filing of the articles of incorporation, if this has in fact been done. Then a draft of the proposed bylaws, as prepared by the organizing committee, is presented and voted upon. The bylaws are discussed and adopted as read or as amended, and each member signs them. According to most state statutes under which membership organizations are organized, the bylaws must be adopted by a majority vote of the members.

The meeting should then proceed to the next item of organizational business. For example, if not previously named in the articles of incorporation, the first board of directors should be elected.

During the initial period of organization, special rules may be adopted limiting the time of, or for, debate. (1 HP Sec. 94.) A resolution limiting debate during this period may take the following form:

> *Resolved*, That until the organization of this body by the election of a chairman, no member shall speak for more than ten minutes on any question, nor shall any member speak more than once on any question; when every member desiring to speak shall have spoken, and after the previous question has been ordered, there shall be no further debate. [1 HP Sec. 94.]

If the members wish to prohibit debate entirely during the period of organization, the resolution may take the following form:

> *Resolved*, That until the election of a chairman, no debate on any subject shall be in order except upon unanimous consent of the members. [1 HP Sec. 95.]

Even in the absence of such special rules, it is well settled that extended debate during the initial meetings on irrelevant matters is out of order. If a member continues to speak on such subjects, the temporary presiding officer may call him to order and put the question to the membership as to whether such individual should be allowed to proceed. (1 HP Sec. 69.)

[4]Hereinafter cited as HP.

Set out below are sample minutes of a first meeting of members following the filing of the articles of incorporation.

MINUTES OF FIRST MEETING OF MEMBERS

The first meeting of the members of [NAME OF ASSOCIATION] was held at [TIME OF DAY] on [MONTH, DAY, YEAR], at [PLACE OF MEETING], in [TOWN, STATE]. The chair called for proof of notice of the meeting, whereupon [NAME OF MEMBER] presented a waiver of notice and consent to hold the meeting signed by all of the members of the association, which waiver and consent was in the following form:

[*Insert copy of waiver of notice and consent to meeting*].

The chair ruled that the meeting was properly called. The chair reported that the articles of incorporation of the association were filed on [MONTH, DAY, YEAR], at [TIME OF DAY] in the office of the Secretary of State of the state of [NAME OF STATE], and presented a copy of said articles of incorporation, which was read, and on motion duly made, seconded, and carried, was directed to be entered in full in the minute book. (See page 00.) A draft of proposed bylaws for the government of the association was presented by [NAME OF MEMBER] and was read to the meeting and discussed section by section and as a whole, and the proposed bylaws were adopted. Each member affixed his signature to the bylaws, and the secretary was instructed to spread the bylaws on the minutes of this meeting.

[*Here insert record of any other business that may have been transacted.*]

There being no further business to come before the meeting, on motion duly made and adopted, the meeting was adjourned.

[SIGNATURE]
Temporary Chairman
[SIGNATURE]
Temporary Secretary

Sec. 14. First Meeting of Board of Directors

As soon as possible after the bylaws have been adopted, the board of directors should hold a meeting to take the necessary steps to make the organization a going concern, ready to begin operations.

Since the first meeting of the board of directors is usually held immediately after the first meeting of the charter members, and there is no established procedure for sending out notice of meetings, each director should sign a "waiver of notice" before the meeting begins. A form for such a notice follows:

WAIVER OF NOTICE OF FIRST MEETING OF BOARD OF DIRECTORS

We the undersigned, being all the directors of [NAME OF
ASSOCIATION], [TOWN], [STATE], hereby waive notice of a
meeting of such directors at [TIME OF DAY] on [DAY OF WEEK,
MONTH, DAY, YEAR], at [PLACE OF MEETING] in [TOWN], [STATE],
for the purpose of electing officers of the association to serve
during the ensuing year and transacting any other business that
may properly come before said meeting.
Witness our signatures, this [DAY] of [MONTH, YEAR].
[SIGNATURES]

At the first meeting of the board, the directors should take up
such business as:

1.   Electing—or planning the election of—the first officers of
the organization.
2.   Designating officers or employees to handle funds and issue
checks.
3.   Selecting a bank to handle the organization's business.
4.   Arranging for the keeping of books and records.
5.   Adopting a form of membership applications.
6.   Arranging for the printing and distribution of copies of the
articles of incorporation and the bylaws.
7.   Securing a location and facility to house the organization.
8.   Arranging for bonding officers and employees in accordance
with bylaws.
9.   Selecting a manager or chief executive.

The minutes of this meeting should be prepared by someone
designated by the temporary chairman to undertake this important
task. Set out below are sample minutes of this first meeting of the
board.

MINUTES OF FIRST MEETING OF BOARD OF DIRECTORS

The first meeting of the board of directors of the [NAME OF
ASSOCIATION, TOWN, STATE], was held at [TIME OF DAY] on
[MONTH, DAY, YEAR], at [PLACE OF MEETING], in [TOWN,
STATE].
Upon convening, [NAME OF MEMBER] was elected tempo-
rary chairman and [NAME OF MEMBER] temporary secretary of the
meeting, and each assumed his office.
The chair called for proof of notice of the meeting, where-
upon [NAME OF MEMBER] presented a waiver of notice and con-

sent to hold the meeting, signed by all the directors of the association, which waiver and consent was written as follows:

[*Insert copy of waiver of notice and consent to holding meeting.*]

Upon roll call of the directors of the association, the following answered present:

[*Record the names of all directors present.*]

The chair ruled that proper and legal notice of the meeting had been given and that a quorum was present, and announced that the meeting was open for transacting business.

The chair stated that the meeting was called for the purpose of electing officers* of the association for the ensuing year and transacting any other business that might properly come before the meeting.

Upon motion duly made, the following officers were elected to serve at the discretion of the board until the time of the first regular meeting of the board to be held as soon as practicable following the first annual meeting of members:

[*Record the names of the officers elected and the title of office.*]

Following the election of the officers, the president took the chair, and the secretary assumed the duties as secretary of the meeting.

Upon motion duly made and carried, the following were appointed members of the executive committee, as provided in the bylaws:

[*Record the names.*]

Upon motion duly made and seconded, the following resolution was adopted:

Resolved, That the executive committee be charged with the following specific powers and duties:

[*State here the specific powers and duties that it is desired to delegate during the period when the directors are not in session, subject to the general direction of the board.*]

Upon motion duly made and seconded, the following resolution was adopted:

Resolved, That the president and secretary be, and they are hereby, authorized to issue certificates of membership† in the form as submitted to this meeting, and each in form as follows:

[*Here insert form. A suggested form appears in Sec. 42* infra.]

---

*Omit if the officers are named in the articles of incorporation.

†If the association is formed with capital stock, the resolution should be changed to authorize the issuance of certificates of stock, and the forms of the certificates should be inserted in the resolution.

Upon motion duly made and seconded, the following resolution was adopted:

Resolved, That the president and secretary be, and they are hereby, authorized to have printed a sufficient number of copies of the articles of incorporation and bylaws, so that a copy thereof may be delivered to each member and each person who may later become a member of the association.

Upon motion duly made and seconded, the following resolution was adopted:

Resolved, That all subscriptions for member capital of the association and marketing contracts with the association, appearing on the list submitted by the secretary, be accepted, and that the president and the secretary be, and they hereby are, directed to carry out the terms and conditions thereof, and to execute all marketing contracts for and on behalf of the association.

Upon motion duly made and seconded, the following resolution was adopted:

Resolved, That [NAME OF BANK] be selected as a depository for the funds of the association.

Upon motion duly made and seconded, the following resolution was adopted:

Resolved, That all checks drawn upon the [NAME OF BANK], for withdrawal of funds of the association on deposit therewith, be signed by the treasurer and countersigned by either the president or the vice-president.

Upon motion duly made and seconded, the following resolution was adopted:

Resolved, That the treasurer is hereby authorized to receive all funds paid into the association, endorse all checks and other media of exchange, and deposit the same to the account of the association in [NAME OF BANK].

Upon motion duly made and seconded, the following resolution was adopted:

Resolved, That the executive committee be, and is hereby, authorized to determine the amount of the bond or bonds that the bylaws specify shall be required of all officers, agents, and employees charged by the association with responsibility for the custody of any of its funds or property, and to see that the bonds, as required, are executed and presented for the approval of the board of directors.

[Similar resolutions should be adopted providing for insuring the property of the association and for adequate insurance covering other contingencies. Any additional business transacted by the board should also be recorded here.]

There being no further business to come before the meeting, on motion duly made, seconded, and adopted, the meeting adjourned.

[SIGNATURE]
Chairman

Sec. 15. Order of Business at Initial Meetings

As suggested above (Sec. 13), the first order of business in the organizing meetings is the election of a chairman and other officers and the adoption of bylaws and rules. If the members wish to open such a meeting with prayer, the prayer should precede the election of the chairman or the adoption of the rules. (1 HP Sec. 99.)

The election of a chairman should precede any correction of the clerk's roll of the members; in this regard, the motion to proceed to the election of a chairman is of higher privilege than a motion to correct the clerk's roll. (1 HP Sec. 22.)

The next order of business is for the chairman or speaker to administer the oath of office to the officers elected. (1 HP Sec. 81.)

The next order of business (after administering the oath of office to the various officers of the organization) is to adopt a system of rules of procedure for the conduct of business before the organization. (1 HP Sec. 81; as to the adoption of rules, see Sec. 43 *infra*.)

Resolutions affecting organizational matters are privileged and take precedence over motions to consider certain business. For example, a resolution that the chairman appoint a certain committee takes precedence over a motion to consider certain monetary matters. (6 Cannon's Precedents[5] Sec. 3.)

Sec. 16. Electing a Presiding Officer

It is difficult, if not impossible, for a membership organization to function without a presiding officer. This need is especially great during its formative or organizational stages. Accordingly, at its initial meeting, the membership should proceed to the election of a presiding officer, who is generally called the president or chairman. And since this election is itself important business, over

[5] Hereinafter cited as CP.

which someone must preside, the members should vest someone with power to act as temporary chairman or as temporary presiding officer. In the case of an organization that has held prior conventions or conferences, this person should be that person who held the office of clerk or secretary during the prior meeting. (1 HP Sec. 64.)

If the organization is meeting for the first time, having no prior existence, the member who calls the meeting to order should ask for nominations from the floor for temporary chairman. The person so elected then becomes the temporary presiding officer. An alternative method, and a simpler one, is to open nominations for temporary clerk or secretary. The person so elected then becomes the temporary chairman or temporary presiding officer, and he presides until the election of a permanent chairman.

In the U.S. House of Representatives, in the event of the unexpected absence of a presiding officer, it is appropriate to move that the member with the longest period of service be appointed on a temporary basis to serve as the presiding officer. This motion may be agreed to by simple majority. (1 HP Sec. 118.)

At the initial meeting, and pending the election of a speaker or chairman, the clerk calls the members to order, calls the membership roll, preserves order and decorum, and decides all questions of procedure subject to appeal to the membership. (Rule III, House Rules Sec. 637.) Language to this effect should be included in the bylaws. In the event that the bylaws do not authorize the clerk to preserve order pending the election of a chairman, the membership may achieve the same objective by special resolution as follows:

> *Resolved*, That until organization of this body by the election of a chairman, the clerk is authorized and empowered to preserve order on the floor, and for that purpose he may exercise the powers ordinarily devolving upon the chairman. [1 HP Sec. 101.]

In exercising his power to decide questions of procedure, the clerk, at the initial meeting, may determine such questions as whether a motion is in order. (1 HP Sec. 65.) He also has the authority, prior to the election of a chairman, to recognize members who wish to address the organization. (1 HP Sec. 74.) Similarly, he may, pending the election of the speaker, in deciding questions of order, determine that a recess pending a demand for the previous question is not in order. (1 HP Sec. 75.)

The clerk's authority as presiding officer of the organization prior to the election of a chairman is not, however, unlimited. It has been ruled, for example, that the clerk may not in that capacity entertain a motion for the referral of certain business to a committee. (1 HP Sec. 78.) In fact, the clerk should not entertain any proposition that is not consistent with organizing the membership into an effective, functioning body. (1 HP Sec. 80.)

If the clerk feels that a decision on a question of procedure is of such magnitude as to be beyond the scope of his authority, he may, pursuant to a motion, put the question to the membership to decide. (1 HP Sec. 68.) For instance, the question of whether a particular motion to table is debatable may be referred by the clerk to the membership for a decision. (1 HP Sec. 70.) And if the clerk, while acting as the presiding officer, refuses to put a question to the membership, a member may rise and put the question from the floor. (1 HP Sec. 67.) Indeed, if the clerk or secretary refuses at any time to exercise the responsibilities of the presiding officer pending the election of the chairman or speaker, a member may rise and move from the floor that such authority be vested temporarily in another member. (1 HP Sec. 64.) Such a motion would take the following form:

> *Resolved*, That [NAME OF MEMBER] be appointed temporary chairman of [NAME OF ORGANIZATION] to serve until the election of a chairman.

—3—

MERGERS AND CONSOLIDATIONS

Sec. 17. In General

Whenever two membership organizations are considering the joining of forces, the difference between a merger and a consolidation must be borne in mind. In a merger, normally, one of the organizations is absorbed by the other, often without changing the name of the surviving organization. In a consolidation, a wholly new organization is created, with a new name, and all of the requirements for the creation of the new organization, including the filing of articles of incorporation, must be complied with.

Although the merger of one membership organization with another is analogous in some ways to the merger of corporations, there are many different and distinct factors to be considered. In the case of corporate mergers, the primary consideration is financial, whereas in the case of a membership organization, the main issue concerns the control over the objectives and operations and activities of the organization that result from the merger.

In a merger of membership organizations, a key issue will involve the voting rights of the respective members of the two organizations. For example, in a merger by an organization of ten thousand members with another organization of five thousand members, the former is likely to emerge with the stronger power base in the event of some dispute arising subsequent to the merger.

Sec. 18. Procedure

Mergers and consolidations between two or more membership organizations give rise to especially difficult procedural problems. Normally, an affirmative vote of the board of directors of each organization will be required, but this should not even be sought until there has been a thorough study of all advantages and disadvantages plus considerable preliminary negotiation.

A special committee should be established to study and report on the problems involved. Summaries of these reports may be given to the members from time to time, since they, too, will ultimately vote on the question. This vote is usually taken at the annual meeting, after much controversy and emotional discussion. No matter how beneficial the merger might appear, no matter how sound its supporting arguments may seem, there will always be those who will oppose it, if only for sentimental reasons. To anticipate this almost inevitable development, the directors should be briefed so that they can provide factually accurate information at the meeting and can combat rumors through visits to key members.

The first step in a merger or consolidation of two membership organizations is the preparation of a letter of intent to merge. This letter is ordinarily signed by the two chief officers of the two organizations. This letter is then distributed to the other officers in each organization, as well as to the respective memberships. This is done, not for the purpose of voting, but to apprise all concerned of the impending merger and to obtain their comments and views.

The second step in either a merger or a consolidation is for the board of directors of each organization to approve the plan for merger by affirmative vote. This is done by resolution.

The third step is for the plan of merger to be submitted to those members of each organization that have voting rights. The plan may be submitted at an annual or at a special meeting of the members, of which written notice must be given. This notice must set forth the proposed plan or contain a summary thereof.

—4—

INCORPORATION, CAPITALIZATION, AND FINANCE

Sec. 19. The Question of Incorporation

Every membership organization should determine at the outset whether it should incorporate. In this regard, the term "corporation" as it relates to membership organizations is frequently misunderstood. If the organization has been incorporated, it has the legal status of a corporation just as any other incorporated business.

Most states have special enabling laws under which membership organizations may incorporate. Incorporation may be brought about under either the general section or the nonprofit section of the state's corporation code. Under these statutes, the law specifies areas of responsibility and procedures to be followed for the different kinds of membership organizations.

Incorporation gives the membership organization a distinct legal standing, with a distinct legal identity, and an established term of existence. Incorporation for the organization has many advantages, the primary one being that members are not personally liable for the debts of the organization after incorporation. (See Sec. 20 *infra*.)

However, it is not necessary that a membership organization be incorporated. If the group is small, and the services to be provided by it are limited in number and complexity, it is possible for it to operate as an unincorporated organization. A decision not to incorporate may also be appropriate where the organization has a limited purpose or has relatively short-term objectives.

An unincorporated organization is roughly equivalent to a partnership. This means that each member is liable for all the debts

31

of the organization. Other disadvantages of the partnership form are that it is more difficult for such an organization to buy or sell land, borrow money, or dispose of assets; under state law, such action may require the approval of all members.

Sec. 20. Advantages and Disadvantages of Incorporation

A membership organization enjoys many advantages through incorporation. In the first place, it becomes a legal entity, which can sue and be sued in its corporate name. In addition, the existence of a membership organization in the corporate form may be perpetual, and is not dependent on the life-span of those persons who created it.

An identifiable legal entity—the corporation—is created, which is separate and distinct from the members as well as the officers of that corporation. As such, it can own property, buy and sell commodities, produce services, make contracts, and undertake financial obligations.

In this regard there is a distinct psychological advantage to be gained from incorporation. The general public, and especially businessmen, are accustomed to dealing with corporations. Banks and other lending institutions are likely to feel more secure in extending credit to a corporation than to a group of individuals.

Another advantage of incorporation is that it shields the organization's officers and members from individual liability in certain areas of litigation. If an agent or employee of an unincorporated organization injures someone negligently while acting within the scope of his authority, the members may be sued individually or together by the injured person. Likewise, if a workman employed by the organization is injured on the job, any claim he might have against the unincorporated association would be a claim against the individual members. On the other hand, if the organization is incorporated, the individual members are shielded from liability in such cases. The corporate entity operates as a barrier between its members and any person to whom the organization is obligated, and it is to that entity that such person must look for compensation.

Incorporation is particularly desirable where the organization is likely to be engaged in either the purchase or the sale of real property. If incorporated, the organization will, of course, act in its own name, whereas an unincorporated organization must act through its members, who may be reluctant to permit real property (with possible tax burdens) to be held in their names.

A disadvantage of incorporation lies in the stricter requirements that are generally imposed on incorporated organizations as distinguished from unincorporated organizations. State laws commonly impose relatively strict requirements on incorporated organizations with respect to the giving of notice of special meetings, amending bylaws, setting minimum quorums for meetings, terminating a member's interest in corporate property when he resigns, and the like. In an unincorporated organization, on the other hand, the members may deal with such matters without considering the requirements of the state corporation statutes.

Sec. 21. Capital Requirements and Needs

Every membership organization needs capital, the amount needed varying with the nature of its activities and the kind of services it performs. Capital is a necessary resource even for those membership organizations that are considered self-sustaining.

Membership organizations need capital if only to establish and maintain themselves. Capital is needed to pay salaries, rent or purchase land, and buy supplies and equipment.

Contributing initial capital is a basic member responsibility. However, the amount invested by a member should not determine the extent of his participation in the activities of the organization, and ordinarily should not be the basis for sharing benefits, at least in nonstock membership organizations.

After capital contributions from members reach a certain level, they can be used as a credit base to obtain supplementary capital from outside credit sources. In this respect, the more initial capital the members supply, the easier it will be to get outside credit. Obtaining at least one half of the initial capital from members is a desirable goal.

Federated membership organizations frequently look to their local affiliates for either initial or supplementary capital. Financial arrangements of this nature are common, particularly where services to individual members are provided primarily by the local affiliates. In such cases it is much easier, of course, to generate capital contributions at the local level. Capital contributions of this nature, made by the local affiliate to the parent organization, should be considered as an investment asset and treated as such.

In raising capital, the organization should attempt to obtain the exact amount needed. An amount smaller or larger than the ideal will cause the organization to be less than efficient in its financial operations.

Sec. 22. Stock Versus Nonstock Organizations

Under the laws of most states, a membership organization may be organized with or without capital stock. The classification of an organization as either (1) stock or (2) nonstock is significant in that it indicates the source of its capital and also discloses the nature of any claim to assets held by the members or investors.

The stock-type organization customarily issues one or more shares of capital stock to members in exchange for their capital contributions. The ownership interests in such an organization are determined by the relative amount of stock owned by each member. In a nonstock organization, on the other hand, the members' claims to the assets of the organization are equal.

If it is a capital stock organization, members are issued stock certificates as evidence of their capital subscriptions. An organization may issue both common stock *and* preferred stock. Some stock organizations issue one share of common stock to a member to show membership, with preferred stock being issued to show additional contributions.

Preferred stock enjoys a preferred position over common stock with respect to dividends and also in the protection it affords investors in the event of dissolution. Hence, it may attract investors, both members and nonmembers alike. This kind of equity capital for a membership organization merits special consideration because it provides a means of spreading ownership among more people without giving up control.

A membership organization need not issue capital stock, even though it obtains capital contributions from its members. Nevertheless, in such a case, some kind of certificate—usually a refund certificate—is issued to show capital contributions of members. Of course, many membership organizations raise their original capital by means of a membership fee, in which case a simple membership certificate is sufficient evidence of the member's capital contribution.

Sec. 23. Sources of Capital or Income

Sources of capital or income for membership organizations may be classified as (1) membership fees, dues, and special assessments, (2) direct investments by members, (3) nonmembers' investments, (4) income-producing operations of the organization, and (5) credit institutions.

Equity capital and creditor capital differ in the nature of the financial interest of the contributor and in the nature of the risk involved.

Equity capital, which is commonly held by such membership organizations as investment clubs and farmer cooperatives, is ownership capital in the real sense. Equity capital is often called risk capital, because losses incurred are absorbed by the owners.

Creditor capital is that being used in the organization other than equity capital. It belongs to others and must be returned to them with interest in accordance with terms agreed to by the organization and its creditors.

Direct investments by members are a significant source of equity capital, as the members in any event have the responsibility for furnishing capital requirements. In some organizations the members invest in equity capital approximately in proportion to the services they use. A nominal rate of return may be paid on equity capital, when justified by net savings.

Sec. 24. Dues

In recent years it has become apparent that membership dues are not the only or even the best source of income for membership organizations. They are criticized on the ground that they are seldom equitable in their application to each member. Flat-rate dues structures are too inflexible, whereas, on the other hand, fluctuating dues schedules are difficult to police. Complicated dues structures tend to be confusing and frequently incur membership displeasure. In addition, it is well known that the collection of dues from members who are delinquent is a sensitive and costly business.

The most common complaint regarding dues is that they are generally too low to cover all programs desired by the membership. Yet if the organization increases its dues, it may find that the rate is too high for the younger member. Even in large organizations, which enjoy weight of numbers to allow smaller dues, the payments themselves are often arbitrary and related to nothing more specific than an out-of-date budget. Thus it is that most organizations find themselves in a fiscal position in which dues are too low to cover the cost of basic services and must be supplemented through other sources of income.

Notwithstanding these criticisms, dues systems are almost

universally in use and are regarded as a constant and generally predictable source on which a membership organization can depend for income. In addition they provide a common ground for membership involvement.

Most membership organizations determine membership dues according to a fixed or flat rate. However, some of them permit dues that fluctuate from member to member, and impose dues based on such factors as a member's total annual volume of sales.

A fixed sum or flat-rate dues structure is generally suitable to professional societies, such as medical and legal associations, where different types of memberships are available. Many bar associations, for example, provide for general membership dues, associate membership dues, and junior membership dues, each being based upon a certain number of years in practice. Such programs are considered relatively inflexible, for only an increase in membership can increase revenues from dues.

In some membership organizations, especially trade associations, the dues structure is a fluctuating one based on guidelines applied in the business world, such as units of production. This system is feasible where the product involved is a homogeneous one with units of approximately equal value. Of course, this type of dues plan is wholly inappropriate for organizations representing multi-product companies or representing more than one field of manufacturing.

Another method for determining a dues system is predicated on the units of equipment or plants owned by a member, and some associations use the number of employees as a dues factor. Assets as a dues base are used almost exclusively by associations representing banking or financial institutions.

Dues structures based on profits, percentages of income, and man-hours of employees are not widely used, primarily because of the confidentiality of such information and because of the complex accounting methods that are required.

Ideally, a dues system for a membership organization should consist of two elements: (1) a dues structure or base and (2) a dues rate. Under such a plan, the organization can adapt to changing conditions within its field of activity or in the economy, and flexibility can be built into the system. It is not necessary that both the dues base and the dues rate be flexible. If the rate is flexible—that is, can be changed easily and frequently—then the organization can select a dues base that remains stable. For example, an organization may base its dues on the units of equipment used by members, but change the rate applied to such units each year.

A dues system tends to become especially inflexible when both the dues structure and the dues rate are written into the bylaws. This is so because the changing of a bylaw may be a difficult and drawn-out procedure. Since the dues structure is seldom changed, it is not as great a problem as where the rate is specified in the bylaws. For this reason, less than half of the nation's membership organizations specify the dues rate in the organization's bylaws. The growing trend is to omit specification of the dues rate in the bylaws.

The board of directors should be given general discretion, subject to specified limitations, as to the revision of the dues base or rate, so that minor changes may be made without being presented to the membership.

The great majority of membership organizations specify both a maximum and a minimum rate in their dues schedule. Of those that specify one or the other, more organizations specify minimum rates than maximum rates.

In most membership organizations, membership dues statements are billed on an annual basis, and some on a monthly basis. Less popular are plans calling for billing members for dues on a quarterly or semiannual basis.

A member who fails to pay his dues within thirty days of notice should be considered delinquent and not in good standing. If subsequent notices are likewise ineffective, services may be suspended as to that particular member. His voting rights may be denied, and his attendance at meetings restricted. Lastly, if the delinquent fails to respond over a period of several months, a final notice should be sent by the board indicating that the member will be dropped from the membership rolls.

Sec. 25. Special Assessments

Special assessments are another form of income for most membership organizations. The difference between assessments and dues lies in the purpose for which the money is used. Money used for general operating expenses is paid by all members and is derived from dues. Assessments are payments made for a specific purpose other than a general operating expense.

Special assessments may be used by a membership organization to finance such programs as research studies, scholarships, legislative programs, public relations activities, and advertising.

Special assessments are generally used to pay for a special nonrecurring project when funds from dues or other sources are unavilable. Special assessments may be levied against a certain class of members when the benefit to be derived therefrom will be enjoyed only by those members.

Special assessments may be mandatory or voluntary. Voluntary special assessments are by far the most popular. In fact, it has frequently been the experience of membership organizations that they are able to raise more funds through voluntary programs than through mandatory ones. Financing can be put on an ability-to-pay basis rather than an enforced basis.

When an assessment is voluntary, members may submit a payment of any size. However, many associations give guidelines for the size of payment they think would be appropriate. This payment may be either a fixed or a fluctuating amount, or it may be predicated on the same base as the dues structure.

Sec. 26. Special Activities and Programs

Sources of capital for a membership organization include income from special activities and programs. Programs with income-producing potential include research activities for members, the sale of supplies and equipment to members, and the offering of design or consulting services to the membership. For example, one membership organization, the National Hardware Dealers Association, will advise members on store location, on store remodeling or construction, and on the ordering and installation of fixtures and equipment. This work is done on either a contract or an hourly-fee basis. Another source of income for this association is derived from promotional and marketing programs provided for the members.

Another important source of income for a membership organization is advertising in and subscriptions to the organization's magazines and journals. Under the revised regulations of the Internal Revenue Service, however, magazines are subject to federal income tax if the overall operation of the magazine is profitable and there is a net income from ads.[1]

For many associations, the most important source of income is from the operation of trade shows and exhibits. In this regard, the IRS has accepted trade show revenues as income related to the exempt function of nonprofit organizations.[2]

Meetings and conventions generate many thousands of dollars

[1]*Nondues Income of Associations* (American Society of Association Executives, 1971), pp. 13, 14.

[2]Ibid., p. 16.

for membership organizations. Among the devices used by organizations to increase income from conventions are registration fees, sale of advertising in convention programs and exhibit directories, convention tours, and sponsorship of events by suppliers and others.

Educational programs are another source of income for most membership organizations, particularly professional membership organizations. For example, a membership organization may put on an annual educational program lasting about one week. Members attend, paying a registration fee of fifty to two hundred dollars. This fee includes texts, work sheets, receptions, and the like. While expenses are substantial, such activities realize a good net return on the total operation.

Another source of income for membership organizations is the so-called deferred-giving program. Under such a program, a member remembers his organization in his will by way of a term life insurance policy. Such policies cost little, pay substantial amounts to the organization, and the premiums therefor are deductible from taxes in the years purchased because of the tax-exempt status of the organization.

Sec. 27. Investments; Revolving Funds

A source of income for many membership organizations is found in the investment of reserve funds. Such investments should be controlled pursuant to discretionary policy decisions of the organization's officers and should not be hampered by bylaw restrictions. The responsibility for them lies not with the membership, but with the organization's officers and chief executives.

Historically, the investment policies of membership organizations have been rigidly conservative, and rightly so in view of the trust relationship between officers and members. Frequently, investments have been placed in government bonds or other holdings offering high liquidity and low risk. In view of the current rate of inflation, and the advisory services and investment experience available, membership organizations should consider investing a larger share of their available funds in equities.

Diversification in investments of reserve funds should be considered where the reserves are relatively large and have remained stable for a number of years. Common stock investments represent a variable source of fluctuating capital which tends to compensate for inflationary tendencies and should be considered in a proper case by an organization's board of directors when the question of investment of cash reserves arises.

Mutual funds represent another useful form of investment, particularly for organizations with relatively small reserves. They offer liquidity and tend to avoid the administrative and accounting problems common to many other forms of investment.

The mere fact that a membership organization makes investments from its reserves will not necessarily violate or disturb the nonprofit status of the organization. Where the investment policy is one of long-term holding and not for quick profits, common stock ownership does not jeopardize an organization's tax status.[3]

Revolving funds are another source of income for most membership organizations. There are many circumstances in which an organization is justified in using reserves as a revolving fund to finance projects that have an income-producing potential extending over a period of several years. Educational or research programs are good examples of such activities. If there is a clear need for a particular project, and a reasonably good chance that it will pay for itself over a period of several years, a membership organization may be wise to underwrite the development cost of the project out of reserves. These reserves can then be repaid over the period when income from the project is being received.

Sec. 28. Financial Controls; Bonds

The board of directors owes a duty to the members to exercise appropriate financial control over the organization's funds. The board and others responsible for the expenditure of organization funds should make certain that moneys designated for special activities or projects be used for the purposes specified. Lawsuits based on the waste or misuse of organization funds are not uncommon.

There are various ways in which a membership organization may control expenditures. An organization may, for example, require that all checks be signed by two persons, and a few of them even require three signatures on checks above a certain amount. Likewise, an organization may in its bylaws place a maximum on expenditures of unbudgeted items which may be made by the organization's chief paid executive without authorization from its officers.

[3]See G. D. Webster, *The Law of Associations* (Washington, D.C.: American Society of Association Executives, 1971).

A bond may be required of any officer who handles the funds of the organization. (1 Hinds' Precedents[4] 253.) This bond should be obtained from a reliable bonding institution. In this regard, it is inappropriate for a member of the organization to be the surety on a bond required of one of its officers. (1 HP Sec. 258.) The amount of the bond generally ranges from $25,000 to $100,000.

Nearly all membership organizations distribute an annual report as well as a financial statement to the membership at least once each year. In addition they furnish their board of directors or other governing body with financial statements on a monthly or at least quarterly basis.

Sec. 29. Accounting Procedures

A membership organization is in serious trouble if it does not have an effective and reliable accounting system. This is necessary, if only for management to function properly.

Since the board of directors has the major responsibility for financial planning and controls, they should familiarize themselves with basic accounting procedures and their uses and applications. A certified public accountant or other qualified specialist should be consulted by the board in setting up a bookkeeping system and, if one is to be used, developing a revolving capital plan. A specialist of this kind is also desirable with respect to the auditing of the organization's books and in preparing and filing income tax reports.

Organizations with well-developed accounting systems may use these so-called double-entry accounting systems. Under this system, each entry is recorded twice. It is particularly helpful to the board, for one set of entries describes those assets of the organization that are being used, and the other set describes the organization's financial interest in (or value of) those assets.

Balance Sheets

A balance sheet is used by a membership organization to show its financial position. If properly prepared, the balance sheet will show the organization's financial status at any given point in time. All of the various assets of the organization, as of a given date, are classified and reported together.

Another column in the balance sheet summarizes the financial interests that the organization has in those assets. In some membership organizations the interests of the members are shown as

[4]Hereinafter cited as HP.

"equity," and financial claims against assets are reported as liabilities.

Of chief interest to the board of directors is the use of the balance sheet to ascertain changes that are taking place in key areas of income or expense. Changes can be observed by comparing items of a balance sheet with comparable items from an earlier period.

Operating Statements

In contrast to the balance sheet, the operating statement provides an overall picture of an organization's operations for a specific period of time. Of special interest to the membership and the board is the operating statement's final figure, showing total net savings.

The operating statement, which should be prepared by the manager under the supervision of the board of directors, should be prepared on a monthly basis. A month-to-month comparison of key items tells the board what is taking place in the organization's operations.

Budgets

The budget of a membership organization is a most important tool in the maintenance of financial stability. The primary function of the budget is to provide for the systematic implementation of the organization's programs and services. This requires careful planning and scrutiny of all operational costs for the forthcoming year. These costs are balanced against the total income from dues and other sources.

Financial Ratios

Membership organizations can use certain financial ratios to appraise the soundness of their financial status. One is the *current ratio*, in which current assets are compared to current liabilities. This ratio measures an organization's ability to pay its current obligations (due within one year) with assets that can be converted to cash within one year (current assets). A ratio of two to one is generally considered desirable.

The member-equity ratio is a measure of long-term financial strength. It is usually stated as a percentage and is the amount of total membership equity in the organization's total assets.

This ratio reveals the "leverage" that members have in the financial structure and, consequently, in the control of the organization. The members should own at least 50 percent of all assets to be assured of financial control. A member-equity figure of 75 percent would be even more desirable, since the risk of losing control would be measurably lessened. A high ratio shows financial strength and stability, which is a desirable goal in the financial management of membership organizations.

The External Audit

Every membership organization should consider having its books audited on an annual basis by an independent auditor. This procedure, known as the external audit, is a periodic verification of the organization's records by an independent auditor.

The external audit is the most effective tool available to the board of directors in controlling the organization's operations. The audit should be made at the close of each fiscal year.

The external audit should be made at the request of the board of directors, not the manager, and the auditor should present his report directly to the board. In this way, the board will have first-hand evidence that the organization's records are in order or, on the other hand, that certain accounts show discrepancies which should be investigated. As trustees of the property of the membership, it is essential that the board have such an independent evaluation. Then, equipped with this information, the board can report to the members on the organization's financial position.

Sec. 30. Financial Reserves

Membership organizations should build up financial reserves. These financial reserves should be large enough to cover operating reserves for such items as depreciation and operating losses.

Primarily, reserves are funds for meeting unforeseen circumstances or for acquiring or building new facilities. When such a need arises, the organization can use its reserves instead of borrowing money or impairing its capital. When the reserves build up to an amount considered adequate, the excess may be revolved out to members, at the discretion of the board, in the same manner as revolving funds. In making such decisions, the board should ascertain whether any local statutes require that the reserves be maintained at a specific level.

The amount of reserves is often stated in the bylaws to be a certain proportion of annual gross income. Thus, the bylaws may require that the financial reserve of the organization be kept at a minimum of one third or one half of annual gross income. Or a bylaw may require that the organization's financial reserve be kept at a minimum of two thirds of the annual gross income or that it be kept equal to its annual gross income.

Although a provision for the distribution of assets to members upon dissolution of the organization is in many ways desirable, such a bylaw provision could adversely affect the organization's nonprofit status. Where this is of concern, a provision may be inserted in the articles of incorporation or the bylaws providing for the distribution of assets at dissolution to those other than members. Thus, the bylaws could give authority to the board of directors to designate some charitable or educational organization to which part or all of the assets would pass upon dissolution. Indeed, it may be desirable to exclude any reference whatever to a plan for distribution of assets on dissolution, thereby avoiding any possibility of a profit-making stigma attaching thereto.

Sec. 31. Tax Considerations

Membership organizations, if properly organized and operated, may claim a tax-exempt status under the provisions of the Internal Revenue Code of 1954. Section 501 (c) (6) of this code is the category under which most business and professional membership organizations fall. This section authorizes an exemption for "business leagues." Other parts of the same section authorize exemptions for organizations classified as "charitable" or "educational." "Social welfare," "agricultural," and "labor" are among the other classifications recognized under this provision of the Internal Revenue Code.

Membership organizations falling within the "business league" section of the statute include the American Medical Association, the American Bar Association, and countless trade associations and chambers of commerce.

The basic requirement in qualifying for a tax exemption is that the organization be "not organized for profit and no part of the net earnings of which inures to the benefit of any private shareholder or individual."[5]

[5]See Section 501 (c) (6) of the Internal Revenue Code of 1954.

In determining whether an organization qualifies for tax-exempt status under this statute, the court will consider whether the organization, though nominally nonprofit, is in reality in direct competition for profit with other taxable businesses.[6] However, a nonprofit membership organization does not lose its tax-exempt status merely because it derives some income from performing limited incidental commercial activities. Thus, a corporation that is organized for religious purposes does not lose its tax-exempt status merely because it receives, as income, alms for masses.[7]

On the other hand, nonprofit membership organizations often undertake activities and programs on behalf of their members that put them in direct competition with commercial enterprises offering the same services or products. When this occurs, the officers of the organization should consider whether its tax liability has been jeopardized under Section 501 (c) (6) and IRS regulations adopted pursuant thereto. In general, such activities must be substantially relevant to the tax-exempt purposes of the organization. If such activities are directly related to the homogeneous characteristics of the members in ways that engender the affinity that binds them together in a voluntary organization, these activities will be regarded as related business activities and not as profit-making activities.

[6]Cf. *Club Garona, Inc.,* v. *U.S.,* 167 F. Supp. 741.

[7]See also *Trinidad* v. *Sagrada Orden,* 263 U.S. 578.

—5—

DRAFTING ORGANIZATIONAL PAPERS; ARTICLES AND BYLAWS

Sec. 32. In General

A number of organizational documents or papers must be prepared in establishing any membership organization. These documents include the following: (1) organizing agreements, (2) articles of incorporation (sometimes called the charter), if needed, (3) bylaws, (4) rules of order, (5) membership applications, and (6) membership certificates.

The two documents required by state law that regulate the operation of incorporated membership organizations are the articles (or certificates) of incorporation and the bylaws. Some membership organizations also have "constitutions," although this is not necessary if both documents mentioned above are legally in existence. A "constitution" in this context does not enjoy the usual characteristics associated with the term itself, and often creates confusion, especially as to the priority to be attributed to the organizing documents.

Organizational documents provide the legal framework within which the organization functions. They must be drawn up with care so as to meet all legal requirements and at the same time provide the kind of organizational structure the founders believe will best suit their needs. Therefore, in drafting these documents, the organizing committee (see Sec. 11 *supra*) should confer with an attorney specializing in such matters as well as an experienced and skilled parliamentarian.

An attorney will be needed not only to draft the organizational documents but also to check the legality of various related papers that might be prepared by its officers or the board of directors. An attorney is also advisable when the organization acquires real property, works out capitalization plans, or borrows money.

The preparation of organizational papers is extremely important, because an organization cannot engage in any activity, handle any commodity, or perform any service unless authorized to do so by its charter (articles of incorporation) and/or bylaws.

The forms set out below (Secs. 34-42) are sample legal documents useful in organizing a membership organization. To a large extent, these forms may be used by organizations with or without capital stock. Appropriate changes are suggested in the text of these forms for organizations operating with capital stock, as well as for other situations where alternate methods of organization and operation are desired. Similarly, if the plan of operation of the organization contemplates differing treatment for nonmembers, or calls for patronage distributions, refunds, and the like, revisions or additional provisions will be necessary.

These forms are general in nature and should in every case be checked by an attorney and modified to conform with applicable state law. In addition, there will usually be many specific needs unique to each organization that will require the preparation of special provisions.

Sec. 33. Purpose Clauses

"Purpose" clauses are an integral and essential component of the organizational papers. If the organization is to be incorporated, the purpose statement should appear in the articles of incorporation, as well as in the bylaws. This statement of purpose should be an affirmative description of the objects for which the organization was created. Many different terms may be used to describe the purpose of the organization in its organizing papers. In many states, the controlling statute provides for the following purposes:

> Charitable; benevolent; eleemosynary; educational; civic; patriotic; political; religious; social; fraternal; literary; cultural; athletic;

scientific; agricultural; horticultural; animal husbandry; and professional, commercial, industrial or trade association . . .[1]

The language adopted is of particular importance, because a membership organization may conduct only those activities authorized in the purpose clauses or incidental thereto. Purpose clauses should therefore be drafted in language sufficiently broad to permit expansion of activities in the future without going through the process of amending the articles of incorporation.

The main purpose clause may be followed by subsidiary or supplemental clauses which are intended to restrict or enlarge upon the main, broadly stated purpose clause. The operations of the organization will be inhibited if the purpose clauses are too narrowly drafted. Hence the most advantageous form is a comprehensive and unrestricted purpose clause.

Where more than one purpose of the organization is listed in the bylaws, a statement should be included indicating that such purposes are neither all-inclusive nor mandatory.

Although generality is preferred over specificity, the need to qualify for nonprofit status may require the insertion of a purpose clause indicating a specific nonprofit motive. A failure to adhere to state requirements in this regard may lead to a denial of nonprofit status.[2]

Sec. 34. Organizing Agreement—Model Form

A model form or organizing agreement is set out below. It should be borne in mind that this form, like all other legal forms of a membership organization, may have to be modified to conform to local law and should be checked by an attorney.

MODEL ORGANIZATION AGREEMENT

The undersigned, hereinafter referred to as "Producer," together with other signers of agreements similar hereto, for the purpose of engaging in [TYPE OF ACTIVITY], propose to organize a cooperative association with [*or without*] capital stock under the laws of [STATUTE] of the state of [NAME OF STATE], as here-

[1]See ABA-ALI Model Nonprofit Corporation Act, adaptations of which can be found in many state codes.

[2]*People* v. *Smith*, 190 Misc. 871, 74 NYS 2d 845.

inafter provided, and in consideration of the premises, hereby agrees for himself and for the express benefit of and for the association to be organized, as follows:

1. The association shall be established with suitable articles of incorporation and bylaws as determined by an organization committee consisting of the following persons:

[*State names and addresses of committee members.*]
This committee may, in the discretion of a majority thereof, increase its membership, fill any vacancy therein, and appoint any committees deemed necessary to conduct the details of its affairs. The committee, or any committee designated by it, may prescribe an organization fee to be paid by each person signing an organization agreement similar hereto and may incur necessary obligations, make necessary expenditures, and take any such action as may, in its discretion, be deemed advisable to further the organization of the association.

2. The bylaws of the association shall provide, among other things, that:

[*Here enumerate the chief provisions that it is proposed shall be contained in the bylaws.*]

3. If, on or before [MONTH, DAY, YEAR], the organization committee is of the opinion that sufficient sign-up has been obtained to enable the association to operate efficiently, the committee shall, by notice to be published in one or more newspapers of general circulation in the area in which those who sign agreements like this one reside, specify a date and place for a meeting. The purposes of such meeting shall be to enable those attending to determine, by majority vote, if a sufficient sign-up has been obtained to justify the formation and operation of the association, and to consider such other business as may be deemed expedient. Notice of the action there taken shall be published in one or more newspapers of general circulation in the area.

4. The organization committee shall keep full, true, and detailed accounts of all receipts and of all expenditures of every kind. It shall have such accounts audited and render a written report thereof to the board of directors of the association when organized, and shall thereupon turn over to the association any balance remaining in its hands free of obligation. If the association is not so organized, such unexpended balance shall be prorated among those who contributed thereto.

5. Producer hereby subscribes for [NUMBER] revolving-fund certificates, each of the face value of [AMOUNT] and agrees to pay therefor as follows: [TERMS OF PAYMENT].

[Note: The provision above is appropriate if the association is to be formed without capital stock. If the association is to be formed with capital stock and is not to use a marketing agreement, the following paragraph is appropriate.]

6. Producer hereby agrees that his signature hereto shall be irrevocable, except as provided herein or in the bylaws of the association, and he so agrees in order to induce other producers to sign agreements like this one for his benefit as well as their own general benefit.

7. Acceptance hereof shall be deemed conclusive upon the mailing, by the association, of a notice to that effect to Producer at his address noted below, and such mailing and notice shall be conclusively established by the affidavit of the secretary of the association.

8. Subject to the terms hereof, Producer agrees to be bound by the terms of the attached marketing agreement.

[Note: Provisions herein relative to marketing agreements should be included only in the case of marketing associations, and if no marketing agreement is used, provisions should be made for dating and for the signature and address of the Producer following Paragraph 7.]

Sec. 35. Articles of Incorporation or Association

An incorporated membership organization comes into existence on the date that its articles of incorporation are filed with the proper state office, usually the office of the Secretary of State. They are necessary, of course, only where the founders have decided to incorporate.

If the founders prefer to operate as an unincorporated organization, which may have its advantages (see Sec. 20 *supra*), they may do so, acting without a corporate charter, but pursuant to bylaws. The founders need only agree among themselves to associate, in which case the agreement may be referred to as the "articles of association." These articles are likewise to be filed with the Secretary of State, at least in some jurisdictions, and comply with other requirements of the law of the state where the organization is being formed.

Articles of incorporation are a statement of the nature and scope of the organization's activities. This statement must be drawn up to conform with the state law. In stating the nature and scope of the organization's activities, it is desirable to do so in broad terms, even though in the beginning the services of the organization may be quite limited. In this way, the founders can anticipate growth and at the same time avoid the procedure of amending the articles at a later date.

The usual requirements for articles of incorporation of not-for-profit membership organizations vary from state to state, but usually include the following:

1.   The purpose or purposes of the organization.
2.   The name of the corporation.
3.   The name and address of each incorporator.
4.   The number and identity of directors constituting the initial board of directors.
5.   Address of the initial business office.
6.   The period of duration.
7.   Any provisions for the regulation of the internal affairs of the corporation (optional).

A specification of capital structure is sometimes required. If the organization is capitalized, the articles of incorporation should show evidence of the minimum paid-in capital. There should also appear in the articles evidence of minimum payments on stock subscriptions if the organization is to issue stock.

The articles of incorporation are filed with the state by the survey committee or the organizing committee. (See Secs. 10, 11 *supra*.) Although many states require only one or more persons to act as incorporators, some states demand a minimum of at least three incorporators. The specific regulations concerning the duties and responsibilities of the incorporators should be determined by reference to local statute.

Sec. 36. Model Articles

Set out below are model articles of incorporation. With some adaptation, they can be drafted to accommodate a wide variety of other kinds of membership organizations.

MODEL ARTICLES OF INCORPORATION

ARTICLES OF INCORPORATION OF [NAME OF ASSOCIATION]

We the undersigned, all of whom are residents and citizens of the state of [NAME OF STATE], engaged in [TYPE OF ACTIVITY], do hereby voluntarily associate ourselves together for the purpose of forming an association, without capital stock, under the provisions of the [STATUTE] of the state of [NAME OF STATE].

ARTICLE I. NAME

The name of the association shall be [NAME OF ASSOCIATION].

ARTICLE II. PURPOSES

The Association is formed for the following purposes:*

To provide or procure for its members any and all goods or services related to [TYPE OF ACTIVITY]; and to perform or make available any other services needed in connection therewith; and to exercise all such powers in any capacity on a cooperative basis.

ARTICLE III. POWERS; LIMITATIONS

Powers. This Association shall have the following powers:

1. To borrow money without limitation† as to amount of corporate indebtedness or liability; to give a lien on any of its property as security therefor in any manner permitted by law.

2. To act as the agent or representative of any patron or patrons in any of the activities mentioned in Article II hereof.

3. To buy, lease, hold, and exercise all privileges of ownership, over such real or personal property as may be necessary or convenient for the conduct and operation of the business of the Association, or incidental thereto.

4. To draw, make, accept, endorse, guarantee, execute, and issue promissory notes, bills of exchange, drafts, warrants, certificates, and all kinds of obligations and negotiable or transferable instruments for any purpose that is deemed to further the objects for which this Association is formed and to give a lien on any of its property as security therefor.

5. To acquire, own, and develop any interest in patents, trademarks, and copyrights connected with or incidental to the business of the Association.

---

*This article should be modified in a manner consistent with local statute to state other specific purposes. Modification will be necessary if the organization wishes to serve nonmembers as well as members.

†In some states the law requires that the maximum indebtedness that may be incurred by a corporation be stated in its articles of incorporation.

6. To cooperate with other similar associations and agencies, for any of the purposes for which this Association is formed, and to become a member or stockholder or such agencies as now are or hereafter may be in existence.

7. To have and exercise, in addition to the foregoing, all powers, privileges, and rights conferred on ordinary corporations and associations by the laws of this State and all lawful powers and rights incidental or conducive to carrying out the purposes for which this Association is formed; and the enumeration of the foregoing powers shall not be held to limit or restrict in any manner the general powers that may by law be possessed by this Association, all of which are hereby expressly claimed.

ARTICLE IV. PLACE OF BUSINESS

The Association shall have its principal place of business in the [NAME OF CITY, COUNTY, STATE].*

ARTICLE V. PERIOD OF DURATION†

The term for which this Association shall exist is [NUMBER OF YEARS] from and after the date of its incorporation.

ARTICLE VI. DIRECTORS

The minimum number of directors of this Association shall be [NUMBER].‡ Of the first elected board of directors, [NAME OF MEMBER] shall be elected for 1 year; [NAME OF MEMBER] for 2 years; and [NAME OF MEMBER] for 3 years; and thereafter all directors shall be elected for 3 years. The names and addresses of those who are to serve as incorporating directors until the first annual meeting of the members or until their successors are elected and qualified are:
[*Insert names and addresses.*]

---

*Some state laws require the inclusion of the name of a resident agent upon whom process may be served.

†If the law under which the association is organized permits perpetual existence this article may read, "This Association shall have perpetual existence."

‡If the statute under which an association is to be incorporated will permit, it is preferable to state in the articles of incorporation only the minimum number of directors that the association will have, and to provide in the bylaws, which may be more easily amended, for the actual number. The provision for staggered terms may not be permitted by the laws of some states. If not, this article should provide that all directors shall be elected each year.

ARTICLE VII. MEMBERSHIP

This Association shall not have capital stock, but shall admit applicants to membership in the Association upon such uniform conditions as may be prescribed in its bylaws. This Association shall be operated on a cooperative basis for the mutual benefit of its members.

The voting rights of the members of the Association shall be equal and no member shall have more than one vote upon each matter submitted to a vote at a meeting of the members.*

The property rights and interests of each member in the Association shall be determined and fixed in the proportion that the patronage of each member shall bear to the total patronage of all the members with the Association. But, in determining property rights and interests, all amounts allocated to each patron or evidenced by certificates of any kind shall be excluded, and, upon dissolution, the equity interests of members and patrons shall be determined as provided in the bylaws. New members admitted to membership shall be entitled to share in the property of the Association in accordance with the foregoing general rule.

In testimony whereof, we have hereunto set our hands this [DAY] of [MONTH YEAR].

> [SIGNATURES]
> [STATE]
> [COUNTY]

Sec. 37. Bylaws

The bylaws of a membership organization are those rules adopted by the members to regulate and manage its business and to set forth the rights and duties of its members. They also define the specific duties and responsibilities of directors, elected officers, and staff.

State laws usually provide that an organization adopt bylaws within a specified time—about one month—after the articles of incorporation are filed. The organizing committee must therefore arrange for a meeting of the officers or incorporators for the specific purpose of adopting the bylaws. (See Sec. 11 *supra.*) The bylaws are usually adopted by the same persons who are identified as incorporators or founders in the articles of incorporation.

---

*If voting on any other basis is permitted by state law and the incorporators desire to provide for another basis, this paragraph should be revised accordingly.

The bylaws are prepared by the organization committee, usually in cooperation with an attorney. The function of the attorney is to ensure that the bylaw provisions comply with federal law as well as the laws of the state in which the organization is based. It is the committee's function to make certain that the bylaw provisions do not conflict with the actual operating procedures and objectives of the organization.

The bylaws set forth the rules for membership, voting and election procedures, the conduct of meetings, and other rules for the operation and management of the organization. These bylaws must be consistent with the articles of incorporation for the organization. Bylaws supplement, and usually are more specific than, the general provisions found in the articles of incorporation. This is permissible. But provisions set forth in the bylaws that are in conflict with one or more provisions in the articles of incorporation are invalid.[3]

The bylaws should specify, as a minimum, the following essential features:

1.   How directors and officers are elected, as well as their number, terms of office, and compensation.
2.   Requirements for membership and the rights and responsibilities of members.
3.   How membership meetings are called and conducted.
4.   Voting procedures.
5.   Time and place of the meetings of the board of directors.
6.   Dates of the beginning and end of the fiscal year.
7.   Approximate time of year, usually by month, when the annual meeting is held.

In setting forth these essential features, the bylaws of the major membership organizations run the gamut in their variations. The provisions of no two sets of bylaws are exactly the same. This is partly because of differences in the legal requirements contained in the statutes under which such organizations are formed or incorporated in the various states. These differences may also reflect divergencies in the objectives and ideas of the organizers.

In drafting bylaws, one is inevitably confronted with the problem of finding an appropriate balance—one that avoids undue rigidity and excessive detail on the one hand, and inadequate or incomplete guideposts on the other. In the final analysis, the pri-

[3]See, for example, *Christal* v. *Petry*, 93 N.E. 2d 450.

mary consideration is to assure a truly democratic, member-controlled organization, but with adequate authority and discretion among the staff and the organization's officers to effectively carry out their duties.

In drafting bylaws, it is as important to know what to exclude from the bylaws as it is to know what to include. The duties of the various officers, for example, may be spelled out in great detail—or in only a few brief sentences. Likewise, it may be desirable to provide for the creation of various committees; and if so, there is a virtually unlimited range of alternatives as to the composition of such committees. Similarly, the manner in which services for members are to be provided can be set forth comprehensively or merely suggested. The manner of nominating candidates to the board of directors (Secs. 62 *et seq. infra*), procedures for voting for officers (Secs. 71 *et seq. infra*), and many other requirements can also be varied to fit the needs and characteristics of each particular organization.

Those who join a membership organization are presumed to know what the bylaws contain. They are bound by their provisions; they may not claim ignorance of them, and liability may result from a failure to observe them. For these and other reasons, a procedure should be established for distributing a copy of the bylaws (or any amendment thereof) to each officer, director, and member. New members should routinely get one copy of the current bylaws along with any other literature regarding the organization.

Specific provisions in the bylaws will prevail over general provisions therein where there is some inconsistency between them.[4]

Sec. 38. Model Bylaws—Trade Association

The organizers of a trade association, just as any other membership organization, should adopt bylaws consistent with their activities and interests. (See Sec. 5 *supra*.)

The model bylaws[5] set out below have been developed from studies of typical bylaws of established and successful trade associations. They are called "model" bylaws because they have been modified and adapted to meet changing needs over a period of

[4]See *New England Trust Company* v. *Penobscot Chemical Fibre Co.*, 142 Me. 286, 50 A. 2d 188.

[5]See also *Basic Operating Policies of Trade and Professional Associations* (Washington, D.C.: Chamber of Commerce of the United States, 1960).

years. It should be obvious, however, that no single "model" can meet all of the differing requirements of the widely varying types of membership organizations that exist in the United States. My intention here is only to illustrate forms of the more important and commonly found bylaws.

Although these bylaws are set forth in terms of trade association practice, the main provisions and bylaws are generally applicable, or at least adaptable, to all membership organizations.

MODEL BYLAWS
TRADE ASSOCIATION

ARTICLE I. NAME

Section 1. The name of the association shall be [NAME OF ASSOCIATION].

Section 2. The principal office of the association shall be in [LOCATION], and it may have such other offices as may from time to time be designated by the Board of Directors.

ARTICLE II. DEFINITION

Section 1. The interests of this association include: [*describe nature and scope of the business or activity to be represented by the association*].

ARTICLE III. OBJECTS

Section 1. The objects of this association shall be:

1. To consider and deal by all lawful means with common problems of management; to secure cooperative action in advancing the common purposes of its members and promote activities enabling the members to conduct themselves with the greatest economy and efficiency.
2. To afford due consideration to and expression of opinion upon questions affecting the members.
3. To cooperate with other organizations.
4. To do anything necessary and proper for the accomplishment of any objects herein set forth or that shall be recognized as proper and lawful objectives.

Section 2. In furtherance of these purposes and objects, but not in limitation thereof, the Association shall have power:

[*Note: Bylaws often list activities of the association. If such provisions are included, they should be neither all-inclusive nor mandatory. Typical activity designations may read as shown below.*]

1. To collect and disseminate statistics and other information.
2. To promote standardization.
3. To conduct investigations and submit reports with reference to [SUBJECT OF CONCERN].
4. To promote activities relating to practices and procedure, such as cooperative buying, technical research, and testing.
5. To conduct promotion activities.
6. To analyze common practices and methods.
7. To advance lawful customs and usages.
8. To promote the arbitration of disputes.
9. To foster and promote sound and equitable employment relations policies.
10. To further training and education of members.
11. To further the reduction of accidents.
12. To analyze financial structures in reference to capital investments and earnings.
13. To promote sound accounting practices and methods.
14. To study financial and related policies with respect to credit, insurance, and obsolescence.
15. To disseminate information of a general economic, social, and governmental character, to analyze subjects relating thereto, and to secure and present the views of the members to other organizations, the government, and the public.
16. To engage in any lawful activities that will enhance the efficient and economic progress of the association and inform the public of its scope and character.

ARTICLE IV. MEMBERSHIP

Section 1. Active. Any person, firm, or corporation engaged in the [TYPE OF INTEREST OR ACTIVITY] is eligible to become an active member of this Association.

Section 2. [*Provision may be made here for other classes of membership such as associate, subscribing, honorary, etc.*]

Section 3. Voting. Each active member firm shall have one vote. Each active member firm or corporation shall appoint and certify to the Secretary of this organization a person to be its representative therein, and who shall represent, vote, and act for the member in all the affairs thereof.

[*Note: If proxy voting is permitted, this should be specifically stated.*]

Section 4. Election of Members. Any person, firm, or corporation eligible to membership under these bylaws may be elected to membership on written application. For such election a majority of votes of the Board of Directors is required.

Section 5. Duration of Membership. Membership in this organization may terminate by death, voluntary withdrawal as herein provided, or otherwise in pursuance of these bylaws. All rights, privileges, and interest of a member shall cease on the termination of membership. Any member may, by giving written notice of such intention, withdraw from membership. Such notice shall be presented to the Board of Directors at the next succeeding meeting of the Board. Withdrawals shall be effective upon fulfillment of all obligations to the date of withdrawal.

[*Note: Provision is sometimes made that all obligations for the fiscal year shall be fulfilled and that action on resignation is withheld until the close of such fiscal period.*]

Section 6. Suspension and Expulsion. For cause, and upon reasonable notice, any membership may be suspended or terminated. Sufficient cause for such suspension or termination of membership shall be violation of the bylaws or any lawful rule or practice duly adopted by this organization, or any other conduct prejudicial to its interests. Suspension or expulsion shall be by two-thirds vote of the entire membership of the Board of Directors.

Section 7. Division of Members. The active members may be divided into such divisions as may be designated by the Board of Directors according to the various branches, such as [*technical, accounting, etc.; members may also be formed into geographical divisions*].

ARTICLE V. DUES

Section 1. The annual dues for each member shall be determined by the Board of Directors.

[*Note: Provision may be made for giving notice to members of dues rates or any changes therein.*]

Section 2. Members who fail to pay their dues [*subscriptions or assessments*] within sixty (60) days from the time the same become due shall be notified by the Secretary or other official of the organization, and if payment is not made within the next succeeding ninety (90) days, shall be reported to the Board of Directors as in arrears, and if so ordered by a majority vote of the Directors present and voting thereon, shall, without further notice and without hearing, be dropped from the rolls and thereupon forfeit all rights and privileges of membership.

ARTICLE VI. MEETINGS

Section 1. Annual. There shall be an annual [*or semiannual or quarterly*] meeting during the month[*s*] of [NAME OF MONTH(S)], unless otherwise ordered by the Board of Directors, for receiving annual reports and the transaction of other business. Notice of such meeting, signed by the Secretary [*or other officer designated by the Board of Directors*], shall be mailed to the last recorded address of each member at least [NUMBER OF] days before the time appointed for the meeting.
[*Note: Incorporated associations must conform to any notice requirements of the state law under which they are incorporated.*]
Section 2. Special. Special meetings may be called by the President or the Board of Directors, or shall be called by the President upon the written request of [NUMBER OF] members of the association. Notice of any special meeting shall be mailed to each member at his last recorded address at least [NUMBER OF] days in advance, with a statement of time and place and information as to the subject or subjects to be considered.
Section 3. Quorum. A majority [*or other number*] of members present at any meeting of the association shall constitute a quorum, and, in case there be less than this number, the Presiding Officer may adjourn the meeting from time to time until a quorum is present.
Section 4. The order of business at meetings shall be as follows:

1. Call of meeting to order.
2. Reading and approval of minutes of previous meeting.
3. Receiving communications.
4. Reports of officers and staff.
5. Reports of committees.
   a. Standing.   b. Special.
6. Unfinished business.
7. New business.
8. Election of Directors.
9. Adjournment.

Section 5. The order of business may be altered or suspended at any regular meeting by a majority vote of the members, a quorum being present.

ARTICLE VII. ANNUAL ELECTION

Section 1. At the annual meeting next held after the adoption of these bylaws, there shall be elected by ballot fifteen directors, five of whom shall be elected for a term of one year, five for two years, and five for three years. [*The number of directors may vary according to the size of the organization.*] At each annual meeting thereafter a number of directors equal to that of those whose terms have expired or are about to expire shall be elected for a term of three years. Any director shall be eligible for reelection. [*A limitation on number of terms of office may be specified.*] Directors shall continue in office until their successors shall be duly elected and qualified.

[*Note: In the event of a divisional organization, provision may be made for representation of the different divisions or sections on the Board of Directors.*]

ARTICLE VIII. BOARD OF DIRECTORS

Section 1. The Board of Directors shall have supervision and control of the affairs of the Association, shall determine its policies or changes therein within the limits of the bylaws, shall actively prosecute its objects, and shall have discretion in the disbursement of its funds.

Section 2. The President and Vice-president(s) [*Treasurer and also Secretary, where appropriate*] shall be members ex officio of the Board, with the right to vote.

Section 3. Meetings. Except that the Board shall have a regular meeting at the time and place of the annual meeting, the Board shall meet upon call of the President at such times and places as he may designate, and shall be called to meet upon demand of a majority of its members. Notice of all meetings of the Board of Directors shall be sent by mail or telegraph to each member of the Board at least fourteen (14) days in advance of such meetings.

Section 4. Quorum. A majority [*or other number*] of the Board shall constitute a quorum at any meeting of the Board. Any less number may adjourn from time to time until a quorum be present.

[*Note: The quorum should be set on the basis most feasible for the particular organization.*]

Section 5. Absences and Vacancies. Any member of the Board of Directors unable to attend a meeting shall, in a letter addressed to the President or Secretary, state the reason for his absence. If a Director is absent from [NUMBER OF] consecutive meetings for reasons that the Board has failed to declare to be sufficient, his resignation may be deemed to have been tendered and accepted. Any vacancies that may occur on the Board by reason of death, resignation, or otherwise may be filled by the remaining members of the Board for the unexpired term.

ARTICLE IX. OFFICERS AND EMPLOYEES

Section 1. The elective officers of this organization shall be a President, Vice-president(s), and a Treasurer. (*A Secretary should be included among the elective officers.*) These officers shall be elected annually by the Board of Directors at a regular meeting held during the annual meeting. Election shall be by ballot, and a majority of the votes cast shall elect.

Section 2. Each elective officer shall take office immediately upon his election and shall serve for a term of [NUMBER OF] year(s) and until his successor is duly elected and qualified.

[*Note: It is important to fix some definite point in time for the election of officers and to specify when they take office.*]

Section 3. Vacancies in any office may be filled for the balance of the term thereof by the Directors at any regular or special meeting.

Section 4. President. The President shall be the chief officer of this organization and shall preside at meetings of this organization and of the Board of Directors. He shall also, at the annual meeting and at such other times as he shall deem proper, communicate matters to the membership or to the Board of Directors as may in his opinion tend to promote the welfare and increase the usefulness of this organization, and shall perform such other duties as are necessarily incident to the office of President or as may be prescribed by the Board of Directors.

[*Note: Provision may be made for a Board Chairman and Executive Committee Chairman other than the President.*]

Section 5. Vice-president(s). The Vice-president(s) may be delegated by the President to perform his duties, in the event of his temporary disability or absence from meetings.

Section 6. Treasurer. The Treasurer shall keep an account of all moneys received and expended and shall make disbursements authorized by the Board and approved by the Secretary and such other officers as the Board may prescribe. He shall make a report at the annual meeting or when called upon by the President. The funds, books, and vouchers in his hands shall, with the exception of confidential reports submitted by members, at all times be subject to verification and inspection of the Board of Directors. At the expiration of his term of office, the Treasurer shall deliver over to his successor, or, in the absence of a Treasurer-elect, to the President, all books, money, and other property.

Section 7. The administration and management of this organization shall be in a salaried staff head, appointed by the President and approved by the Board. He shall have the title of Executive Director or such other title as the Board shall from time to time deem desirable. Subject to the President and the Board, he shall employ and may terminate the employment of members of the staff.

Section 8. Secretary. There shall be a Secretary who shall be appointed by the Board of Directors, to serve at the pleasure of the Board. [*Or he may be an elected officer, as noted above.*] It shall be his duty to give notice of and attend all meetings of this organization and all committees and keep a record of their proceedings; to keep a list of members; to collect annual dues and subscriptions and pay them over to the Treasurer; to prepare an annual report of the transactions and condition of this organization, and generally to devote his best efforts to advancing its interests.

[*Note: Because certain duties of the Secretary may be delegated to a salaried staff head as provided for in Section 7, many of the specific duties shown for the Secretary may be deleted or modified.*]

Section 9. Bonding. The Secretary and Treasurer, or any other person entrusted with the handling of funds or property, shall, at the discretion of the Board of Directors, furnish, at the expense of the organization, a fidelity bond approved by the Board, in such a sum as the Board shall prescribe.

[*Note: Limitations may be specified as to the number of terms of office of elected officers.*]

ARTICLE X. COMMITTEES

Section 1. The President, subject to the approval of the Board of Directors, shall annually appoint such standing or special committees or subcommittees as may be required by the bylaws or as he may find necessary.

[*Note: Provision may be made in the bylaws for certain specific standing committees.*]

Section 2. Executive Committee. There shall be elected annually by the Board of Directors [NUMBER OF] member(s) who, with the President, Vice-president(s), and Treasurer, shall constitute an Executive Committee. They may exercise the powers of the Board of Directors when the Board of Directors is not in session, reporting to the Board of Directors thereon at the succeeding meeting. [NUMBER OF] members shall constitute a quorum for the transaction of business.

[*Note: Where several directors other than designated officers are to serve on an Executive Committee it may be preferable to provide that this committee be appointed by the President, with approval of the Board, rather than to elect it.*]

Section 3. Committee on Nominations. The Board of Directors shall appoint a nominating committee of [NUMBER OF] persons to nominate candidates for the Board of Directors. The committee shall notify the Secretary, in writing, at least thirty (30) days before the date of the annual meeting, of the names of the candidates it proposes, and the Secretary shall mail a copy thereof to the last recorded address of each member at least twenty (20) days before the annual meeting.

[*Note: Limitations may be imposed as to the eligibility of certain persons, such as officers or directors, to serve as members of the nominating committee. It may also be specified that the committee be elected, rather than appointed, and be given the power to nominate officers as well as directors.*]

Section 4. Independent Nominations. Nominations for Directors may also be made, endorsed with the names of not less than [NUMBER OF] members of the Association, if received by the Secretary at least [NUMBER OF] days prior to the annual meeting of the Association for immediate transmittal by him to the members.

[*Note: Nominations may also be made from the floor at an annual meeting unless specifically precluded.*]

ARTICLE XI. FISCAL YEAR

Section 1. The fiscal year shall commence on [DATE] and shall end on [DATE] of each year.

ARTICLE XII. SEAL

Section 1. The Association shall have a seal of such design as the Board of Directors may adopt.

ARTICLE XIII. AMENDMENTS

Section 1. These bylaws may be amended, repealed, or altered, in whole or in part, by a majority (*or two-thirds*) vote at any duly organized meeting of this organization; provided that a copy of any amendment proposed for consideration shall be mailed to the last recorded address of each member at least thirty (30) days prior to the date of the meeting.

[*Note: The authority to make amendments may be vested in the Board of Directors; or it may be specified that member action can be required on an amendment only if it has been proposed by the Board of Directors.*]

Sec. 39. Model Bylaws—Cooperatives

Set out below are model bylaws that are intended for a cooperative. With some modification, these bylaws would be suitable for many other membership organizations and a variety of other types of cooperatives. The bylaws should be carefully checked for consistency with state laws and the articles of incorporation.

ARTICLE I. MEMBERSHIP

Section 1. Qualifications. Any person, firm, partnership, corporation, or association, who is a [TYPE OF INTEREST OR ACTIVITY] and who pays such membership fee and meets such other uniform conditions as may be prescribed by the Board of Directors (hereinafter called the Board), may become a member of this Association. This Association shall issue a certificate of membership to each member which shall be in such form as may be prescribed by the Board but shall not be transferable.

Section 2. Suspension or Termination. If, following a hearing, the Board shall find that a member has ceased to be an eligible member, it may suspend his rights as a member or terminate his membership. Upon termination of membership in the Association, all rights and interests of such member in the Association shall cease. No action taken hereunder shall impair the obligations or liabilities of either party under any contract with the Association, which may be terminated only as provided therein.

ARTICLE II. MEETINGS OF MEMBERS

Section 1. Annual Meeting. The annual meeting of the members of this Association shall be held in [CITY, STATE], at [TIME OF DAY] on the [NUMBER OF] day of [MONTH] of each year, or on any date that the Board shall designate at least thirty (30) days in advance of the date specified above.

[*Note: A delegate system of member representation may be used at the annual meeting, with delegates elected at district meetings by members.*]

Section 2. Special Meetings. Special meetings of the members of the association may be called at any time by order of the Board, and shall be called at any time upon written request of at least [PERCENT] of the members, provided, however, that in no case shall the required number of signatures to such a request be less than [NUMBER ( )]. The request shall state the time, place, and object of the meeting.

Section 3. Notice of Meetings. Written or printed notice of every regular and special meeting of members shall be prepared and mailed to the last known address of each member not less than thirty (30) days before such meetings. Such notice shall state the object or objects thereof and the time and place of meeting. No business shall be transacted at special meetings other than that referred to in the call.

Section 4. Voting. Each member shall be entitled to only one vote upon each matter submitted to a vote at a meeting of the members. Voting by proxy or cumulative voting shall not be permitted.

Section 5. Quorum. Ten percentum of the total number of members, present in person, shall constitute a quorum. If less than a quorum is present at any meeting, a majority of those present in person may adjourn the meeting from time to time without further notice.

Section 6. Order of Business. The order of business at the annual meeting shall be:

1. Determination of quorum.
2. Proof of due notice of meeting.
3. Reading and disposition of minutes.
4. Annual reports of officers and committees.
5. Unfinished business.
6. New business.
7. Election of Directors.
8. Adjournment.

ARTICLE III. DIRECTORS AND OFFICERS

Section 1. Number and Qualifications of Directors. The Association shall have a Board of [NUMBER OF] Directors. Each Director shall be a member in good standing of this Association. No person shall be eligible for the office of Director if he is in competition with or is affiliated with any enterprise that is in competition with the Association. If a majority of the Board finds at any time following a hearing that any Director is so engaged or affiliated, he shall thereupon cease to be a Director.

Section 2. Election of Directors. At the first annual meeting of the members of this Association, Directors shall be elected to succeed the incorporating Directors. [NUMBER OF] Directors shall be elected for 1 year; [NUMBER OF] Directors for 2 years; and [NUMBER OF] Directors for 3 years. Thereafter each Director shall be elected for 3 years. At least two candidates shall be nominated for each directorship. All Directors shall be elected by secret ballot, and the nominee receiving a majority or plurality of votes shall be elected.

[*Note: Many cooperatives find it desirable to use a nominating committee. The following language may be included as a separate section:* "Section —. Nominations. The Board shall appoint, not less than thirty (30) days nor more than sixty (60) days before the date of a meeting of the members at which Board members are to be elected, a committee on nominations consisting of [NUMBER OF] members who shall be selected from different sections so as to insure equitable representation. No officer or member of the Board may serve on such committee. The committee shall prepare and post at the principal office of the Association at least twenty (20) days before the meeting a list of nominations for Board members which shall include at least two candidates for each Board position to be filled by the election."]

[*Note: If the Association wishes to select Directors by districts, it is suggested that Article III, Section 2, might read as follows:* "The incorporating Directors shall serve until the first annual meeting of the members or until their successors shall have been elected and qualified. The incorporating Directors shall divide the territory served by the Association into [NUMBER OF] districts on the basis of geographic areas in which the number of members or the volume of business done with the Association is approximately the same. Each year the Board shall establish a redistricting committee to include one member other than a Director from each district. The redistricting committee shall meet at least one hundred and twenty (120) days prior to the annual meeting and may redistrict the territory as may be deemed advisable. A map and description of the current districts shall be maintained in the principal office of the Association. The Board shall determine the time and place within each district for meetings to nominate Directors."]

Section 3. Election of Officers. The Board shall meet within [NUMBER OF] days after the first election and within [NUMBER OF] days after each annual election and shall elect by ballot a President, Vice-president, Secretary, and Treasurer [*or a Secretary-Treasurer*], each of whom shall hold office until the election and qualification of his successor unless earlier removed by death, resignation, or for cause. The President and Vice-president only need be members of the Board. Vacancies in such offices shall be filled by the Board through election by ballot.

Section 4. Vacancies. Whenever a vacancy occurs on the Board, other than from the expiration of a term of office, the remaining Directors shall appoint a member to fill the vacancy until the next regular meeting of the members.

Section 5. Board Meetings. In addition to the meetings mentioned above, regular meetings of the Board shall be held [MONTHLY, QUARTERLY, OR SEMIANNUALLY] or at such other times and at such places as the Board, by a majority of its members, may determine.

Section 6. Notice of Board Meetings. Oral or written notice of each meeting of the Board shall be given each director by or under the supervision of the Secretary not less than forty-eight (48) hours prior to the time of the meeting, but such notice may be waived by all the Directors, and appearance at a meeting shall constitute a waiver of notice thereof.

Section 7. Compensation. The compensation, if any, of the members of the Board and of the executive committee shall be determined by the members of the Association at any annual or special meeting of the Association.

Section 8. Quorum. A majority of the Board shall constitute a quorum at any meeting of the Board.

ARTICLE IV. DUTIES OF DIRECTORS

Section 1. General Powers. The Board shall direct the business and affairs of the Association and shall exercise all of the powers of the Association except such as are conferred upon or reserved to the members by law, the articles of incorporation, or these bylaws. The Board shall adopt such policies, rules, and regulations not inconsistent with law, the articles of incorporation, or these bylaws, as it may deem advisable.

Section 2. Employment of Manager. The Board shall have power to employ a Manager, define his duties, and fix his compensation.

Section 3. Bonds and Insurance. The Board shall require the Manager and all other officers, agents, and employees charged by the Association with responsibility for the custody of any of its funds or property to give adequate bonds. The Board shall provide for the adequate insurance of the property of the Association, or property that may be in the possession of the

Association, or stored by it, and not otherwise adequately insured, and in addition adequate insurance covering liability for accidents to all employees and the public.

Section 4. Accounting System. The Board shall have installed and maintained an adequate system of accounts and records. At least once in each year the Board shall obtain the services of a competent and disinterested public auditor or accountant, who shall audit the books and accounts of the Association and render a report in writing thereon, which report shall be submitted to the members of the Association at their annual meeting. This report shall include a balance sheet and an operating statement for the fiscal period under review.

ARTICLE V. DUTIES OF OFFICERS AND MANAGER

Section 1. Duties of President. The President shall (1) preside over all meetings of the Association and of the Board, (2) call special meetings of the Board, (3) perform all acts and duties usually performed by an executive and Presiding Officer, and (4) sign all membership certificates and such other papers of the Association as he may be authorized or directed to sign by the Board; *provided, however*, that the Board may authorize any person to sign any or all checks, contracts, and other instruments in writing on behalf of the Association. The President shall perform such other duties as may be prescribed by the Board.

Section 2. Duties of Vice-president. In the absence or disability of the President, the Vice-president shall perform the duties of the President.

Section 3. Duties of Secretary. The Secretary shall keep a complete record of all meetings of the Association and of the Board and shall have general charge and supervision of the books and records of the Association. He shall sign all membership certificates with the President and such other papers pertaining to the Association as he may be authorized or directed to sign by the Board. He shall serve all notices required by law and by these bylaws and shall make a full report of all matters and business pertaining to his office to the members at the annual meeting. He shall keep the corporate seal and affix it to all papers requiring a seal. He shall keep complete membership records. He shall make all reports required by law and shall perform such other duties as may be required of him by the Association or the Board.

Section 4. Duties of Treasurer. The Treasurer shall perform such duties with respect to the finances of the Association as may be prescribed by the Board.

Section 5. Duties of Manager. The Manager shall perform

such duties and shall exercise such authority as the Board may from time to time vest in him. Under the general supervision of the Board, the Manager shall have general charge of the ordinary and usual business operations of the Association. He shall render annual and other statements in the form and in the manner prescribed by the Board.

ARTICLE VI. EXECUTIVE COMMITTEE AND OTHER COMMITTEES

Section 1. Powers and Duties. The Board may, in its discretion, appoint from its own membership an executive committee of [NUMBER OF] members, determining their tenure of office and their power and duties. The Board may allot to such executive committee all or any stated portion of the functions and powers of the Board, subject to the general direction, approval, and control of the Board. Copies of the minutes of any meeting of the executive committee shall be mailed to all Directors within seven (7) days following such meeting.

Section 2. Other Committees. The Board may, in its discretion, appoint such other committees as may be necessary.

ARTICLE VII. MEMBERSHIP CERTIFICATES

The Board shall cause to be issued appropriate certificates of membership.

ARTICLE VIII. OPERATION AT COST; PATRONS' CAPITAL

The Association shall at all times be operated on a cooperative service-at-cost basis for the mutual benefit of its patrons. No interest or dividends shall be paid by the Association on any capital furnished by its patrons.

[*Note: Article VIII is suitable for an association organized on a nonstock basis serving members only. If the association issues stock or serves nonmembers and it is intended that members and nonmembers be treated alike in patronage distributions, provisions accommodating the desired plans should be added.*]

ARTICLE IX. DISSOLUTION; PROPERTY INTERESTS OF MEMBERS

Upon dissolution, after all debts and liabilities of the Association shall have been paid, and all capital furnished through patronage shall have been retired without priority on a pro rata basis, the remaining property and assets of the Association shall be distributed among the members and former members in the proportion that the aggregate patronage of each member bears to the total patronage of all such members, unless otherwise provided by law.

[*Note: If the association is formed with capital stock, this article may be changed to read as follows:* "Upon dissolution, after (1) all debts and liabilities of the Association shall have been paid, (2) the par value of stockholders' shares returned, and (3) all capital furnished through patronage shall have been retired without priority on a pro rata basis, the remaining property and assets of the Association shall be distributed among the members and former members in the proportion that the aggregate patronage of each member bears to the total patronage of all such members, unless otherwise provided by law."]

ARTICLE X. UNCLAIMED MONEY

A claim for money against the Association shall be subject to the provisions of this article whenever the Association is ready, able, and willing to pay such claim, and has paid or is paying generally claims arising under similar circumstances, but payment of such claim cannot be made for the reason that the Association does not know the whereabouts or mail address of the one to whom it is payable or the one entitled to payment.

If such claim be not actually paid within a period of [*insert here a period of time equal to the applicable state statute of limitations with respect to claims of this class*] after becoming payable as herein provided, the Association shall remove the claim as a liability on its books; provided that no such removal shall be made unless at least thirty (30) days prior thereto the Association shall have sent by registered United States post, with a return receipt requested, a written notice of the proposed removal, addressed to the person appearing from the Association's records to be entitled to payment of such money at the last address of such person shown by the records of the Association.

If any such claim be removed of record after giving such notice, the claim shall be deemed extinguished, but the Association shall continue to maintain a memorandum record of such claim and shall pay the principal amount thereof without interest to any claimant who subsequently establishes to the satisfaction of the Association his right to receive payment.

Any and all amounts recovered by the Association pursuant to this article, after deducting therefrom the amount of any taxes payable thereon, shall be placed in a special account. Any claim paid after the expiration of the period of years herein specified shall be deducted from such account.

ARTICLE XI. FISCAL YEAR

The fiscal year of the Association shall begin on the first day of January of each year and shall end on the thirty-first day of December of the same year.

[*Note: If other than the calendar year is selected, this article might read:* "The fiscal year of the Association shall commence on the first day of [MONTH] each year and shall end on the last day of [MONTH] of the following year."]

We the undersigned, being all of the incorporators and members of [NAME OF ASSOCIATION], do hereby assent to the foregoing bylaws and do adopt the same as the bylaws of said Association; and in witness whereof, we have hereunto subscribed our names, this [MONTH, DAY, YEAR].

[SIGNATURES]

Sec. 40. Model Bylaws—Political Action Committees

The organizers of a political action committee should adopt bylaws consistent with the rules governing such organizations (see Sec. 8 *supra*) just as any other membership organization. Model bylaws[6] for such a committee are set out below.

ARTICLE I. NAME

The name of this organization shall be the [NAME] Political Action Committee, a nonprofit political organization of the [NAME OF] industry.

ARTICLE II. PURPOSE

The purpose of the [NAME] Political Action Committee shall be to promote the private enterprise system in the United States, and to raise funds for this purpose, and from such funds to make contributions to those persons in political work without regard to party affiliation who, by their acts, have demonstrated their belief therein.

ARTICLE III. REGULATION

The regulation of the business and conduct of the affairs of this [NAME] Political Action Committee shall be determined by

[6]See also G. D. Webster, *The Law of Associations* (Washington, D.C.: American Society of Association Executives, 1971), p. 459.

these bylaws and by rules that, from time to time, shall be adopted.

ARTICLE IV. OFFICE

The principal office of the [NAME] Political Action Committee shall be located in [CITY, STATE].

ARTICLE V. TRUSTEES

Section 1. The management of the [NAME] Political Action Committee shall be vested in three executive trustees who shall serve at the pleasure of the contributors. The initial executive trustees shall be: [*insert names*].

Section 2. The executive trustees shall appoint from among the contributors a minimum of five advisory trustees to serve at the pleasure of the executive trustees. Such advisory trustees shall advise the executive trustees, but shall not be voting trustees.

Section 3. The executive trustees shall elect such officer, or officers, and appoint such employees as they determine necessary to carry out the purpose of the [NAME] Political Action Committee.

Section 4. The executive trustees shall appoint an Executive Secretary, who shall perform the administrative functions for the executive trustees.

ARTICLE VI. OPERATIONS

Section 1. There shall be an annual meeting of the [NAME] Political Action Committee which shall be at a place convenient to the contributors. Such meetings shall be called by the Executive Secretary.

Section 2. These bylaws may be amended by the unanimous consent of the executive trustees in order to fulfill the purposes of the [NAME] Political Action Committee.

We approve and adopt these bylaws of the [NAME] Political Action Committee and confirm the appointment of Mr. [NAME OF MEMBER] as Executive Secretary and Treasurer to serve at the pleasure of the executive trustees.

[SIGNATURES]

Adopted: [DATE]

Sec. 41. Membership Applications

The membership application form has four main parts: (1) a statement of the desire of the applicant to become a member of the organization; (2) the signature of the applicant; (3) a statement of acceptance of the applicant; (4) the signatures of the president and/or the secretary of the organization.

The membership application should not be considered a mere formality. It is important that the organization have a properly completed membership application from each member. An invalid membership application may result in a challenge to the member's right to vote or other privilege, with consequent embarrassment for all concerned. The membership application, signed by the member and approved by one or more officers, is the best evidence that he is actually a member.

Set out below is a model form for a membership application.

MEMBERSHIP APPLICATION

I hereby apply for membership in [NAME OF ASSOCIATION] and agree to abide by the articles of incorporation and bylaws of said Association, now or hereafter in effect, copies of which have been presented to me for my inspection. After my membership shall have been in effect one year from the date of its acceptance by the Association, either party hereto may terminate it in any year on the last day of the anniversary month in which this agreement was so accepted by notifying the other party in writing of this intention, such notice to be given between the first and fifteenth of the month immediately prior to the effective date of termination. If neither of the parties hereto so notifies the other, it is hereby mutually agreed that this shall constitute conclusive evidence that the parties hereto have renewed this agreement for another year.

Date_____ , 19_____

    Signature_____

        Name_____ [*printed*]

Address_____

Social Security No._____ County_____

Accepted this_____day of_____, 19_____

             _____ , Inc.

        By _____ , Pres.

        By _____ , Sec.

Sec. 42. Membership Certificates

On his acceptance into the organization, each member is issued a certificate as evidence that he is entitled to all of the rights, benefits, and privileges of the membership.

Some organizations supplement the membership certificate,

where appropriate, with a revolving fund certificate. A revolving fund certificate is the member's receipt for certain capital contributions that will eventually revolve back to him. In the meantime, they are retained and used as capital by the organization.

Set out below is a sample form of the membership certificate widely in use among membership organizations.

MEMBERSHIP CERTIFICATE

No._____

This certifies that_____ of_____ , is a member of_____ Association and is entitled to all of the rights, benefits, and privileges of the Association.
Dated_____

_____(President)

_____(Secretary)

Sec. 43. Amendments and Repeals

Most membership organizations find it necessary to amend their bylaws and other organizational papers as they grow and as their activities become more diversified. This is particularly true of membership organizations during the first years of their existence. It is during this time that the methods and operating procedures of an organization generally undergo substantial change. In fact, unless the bylaws are amended, it may develop that the organization's operating procedures are in conflict with its organizational papers.

It is therefore of utmost importance that the directors of every membership organization set aside time for the review of their bylaws once each year. In this way, they will be prepared to propose recommended amendments at the appropriate time, thereby enabling the organization to be responsive to changing conditions. Serious problems can arise if the directors fail to do this, for no organization can engage in any activity unless it is authorized to do so by its charter and bylaws.

The power to alter, amend, or repeal the bylaws lies primarily with the membership as a whole, but this power may be delegated to the board of directors unless prohibited by the bylaws or the articles of incorporation.

The procedure for amending an organization's founding documents should be set forth in the bylaws and is also governed to some extent by state statute. Any legal requirements, such as the giving of advance notice of the proposed change to the membership, must be strictly complied with.

In many states the amendment or repeal of an organization's articles of incorporation is regulated by law. Some statutes list the purposes for which they may be amended and set forth minimum vote requirements. A two-thirds vote of the membership is common.[7]

A review of these statutes compels the obvious conclusion that it is easier to change or amend a bylaw than a certificate of incorporation. And, in practice, certificates of incorporation are rarely changed, whereas bylaws are changed with relative frequency. Accordingly, those responsible for drafting organizational documents should see to it that, if possible, provisions likely to undergo subsequent change be placed in the bylaws.

Amendments to the bylaws are ordinarily proposed at the annual meeting of an organization, but such amendments may be offered any other time if permitted by the bylaws. The board of directors should have the power to amend the bylaws quickly, particularly in an emergency situation.

Proposed amendments, together with supporting arguments, should be circulated to the membership and to the organization's officers and staff well in advance of the meeting in which they are likely to be voted on. Copies should be shown to the parliamentarian and other legal advisers so that any legal or technical questions can be resolved ahead of time. Advance circulation of amendments also enables the members to vote more intelligently on them and tends to generate wider support for an amendment than it would otherwise have.

Any notification to the membership of a proposed change in a bylaw should indicate the exact nature and wording of the amendment and state the reasons therefor. Advance disclosure of this nature is frequently required by state law.

A bylaw is sometimes amended by custom—without formal proceedings—as where the organization adopts a practice contrary to an adopted bylaw in which the membership acquiesces over a long period, or where there is consistent disregard or nonuse of a bylaw by the board of directors, with membership acquiescence.[8]

[7]See ABA-ALI Model Nonprofit Corp. Act, Secs. 35, 36.

[8]See in re *Ivey & Ellington*, 28 Del. 298, 42 A. 2d 508.

—⑥—

PARLIAMENTARY RULES

Sec. 44. Generally; Model Rules

Written rules of order should be adopted by a membership organization, usually by majority vote, to regulate the conduct of its meetings. These rules—also called standing rules—deal with such subjects as the election of officers, calling up business for consideration at the meeting, determining the presence of a quorum, hearing motions, maintaining order, putting matters to a vote, and adjournments.

Membership organizations have broad discretion in the adoption of such rules. A legislative assembly is constitutionally empowered to determine its rules of proceedings. It may not by its rules ignore constitutional restraints or violate fundamental rights, and there should be a reasonable relation between the mode or method of proceeding established by the rule and the result that is sought. But within these limitations all matters of method are open to its determination, and it is no impeachment of the rule to say that some other way would be better, more accurate, or even more just. It is no objection to the validity of a rule that a different one has been prescribed and in force for a length of time. The power to make rules is not one that once exercised is exhausted. It is a continuous power, always subject to be exercised by the assembly, and within the limitations suggested, absolute and beyond the challenge of any other body or tribunal.[1]

Standing rules are usually drafted for a particular organization by a committee created for that purpose, commonly called the Rules Committee. This committee will generally begin with a set of model rules, such as those set out below. The committee will then adapt and reshape them to suit the needs of their own organization.

[1]*United States* v. *Ballin* 144 U.S. 1, 5 (1892).

When the committee has finished its proposed draft of standing rules, it submits the draft to the membership for a vote along with a report of the committee. This report may set forth some of the arguments for or against particular rules and should state the recommendations of the committee as to the adoption of the rules. The question as to the adoption of rules is customarily presented to the membership after the election of the presiding officer. (1 Hinds' Precedents[2] Sec. 93.)

In some membership organizations it is the practice to adopt a new set of standing rules for each annual meeting. Where this is the practice, a member may move that the rules that governed the organization at its prior convention or annual meeting, so far as applicable, be the rules that govern its proceedings during the pending meeting. (1 HP Sec. 67.)

There is a widespread need for a compilation of modern, simple, uniform rules of parliamentary procedure, *based on the law*, that can be adapted for use by any membership organization, legislative or nonlegislative, large or small. Many authorities have pointed out that the parliamentary reference works used most widely today are in fact not based on parliamentary law. This is not entirely unexpected; as has been pointed out by John Waldeck in his unpublished manuscript on parliamentary procedure, most of the leading works and articles on parliamentary procedure in modern times have been written, not by lawyers, but by laymen with backgrounds as varied as army general, WAC colonel, professor of public speaking, psychiatrist, veterinarian, sociologist, priest, and lawyer's wife.[3]

The courts, in resolving disputes over parliamentary procedures, have followed judicial decisions and have rejected the opinions of commentators as not binding.[4]

It is thus clear that a membership organization following a text not based on the law has no assurance that its actions will be upheld by the courts.[5]

These texts have also been criticized on the ground that they

[2] Hereinafter cited as HP.

[3] See John Waldeck, "Parliamentary Procedure for Non-profit Organizations," Cleveland-Marshall Law School, 1965.

[4] See *Abbey Properties Co., Inc.*, v. *Presidential Insurance Co.*, 119 So. 2d 74.

[5] See Paul Mason, "The Legal Side of Parliamentary Procedure," *Today's Speech* (Nov. 1956), p. 9.

are unnecessarily complex and technical[6] and as being replete with archaic terminology.[7]

It is hoped that the rules which follow will fill the need for a universally adaptable set of modern, easy-to-understand rules of order. They are based on the rules in effect in the U.S. House of Representatives; each has been modified or adapted herein so as to be of general applicability.[8] The House Rules have withstood the test of time for nearly two hundred years and have been invoked repeatedly in resolving procedural disputes among the members. These rules (and the thousands of rulings by presiding officers construing them) have been followed by the courts as well as many membership organizations, both legislative and nonlegislative, here and abroad.

[6]Richard Givens, "The Landrum-Griffin Act and Rules of Procedure for Union Meetings," 12 *Labor Law J. 477* [1961].

[7]Howard L. Oleck, *Non-Profit Corporations, Organizations, and Associations*, 2d ed. (Englewood Cliffs, N.J.: Prentice-Hall, 1965), pp. 547-551.

[8]See Lewis Deschler, *House Rules and Manual* (Washington, D.C.: U.S. Government Printing Office, 1973).

MODEL RULES OF PARLIAMENTARY PROCEDURE

RULE I. DUTIES OF THE PRESIDING OFFICER

1. The Presiding Officer shall take the chair at every meeting precisely at the hour to which this organization shall have adjourned at the last sitting and immediately call the members to order. On the appearance of a quorum, the Presiding Officer, having examined and approved the minutes of the proceedings of the last day's sitting, shall announce his approval of the minutes, and unless, in his discretion, he orders the reading thereof, they shall be considered as read. However, it shall then be in order to offer one motion that the minutes be read; such motion is of the highest privilege and shall be determined without debate. See Rule I Clause 1, House Rules. Generally, as to the Presiding Officer, see 2 Hinds' Precedents[1] Ch. 44 and 6 Cannon's Precedents[2] Ch. 177. See also 1 HP Secs. 104-9 (fixing hour of meeting by standing order); 6 CP Sec. 624 (making a point of no quorum before meeting is completed); 4 HP Sec. 2760 (motions to amend the Journal).

2. He shall preserve order and decorum, and, in case of disturbance or disorderly conduct, shall take such action as is necessary to restore order. See Rule I Clause 2, House Rules; see also 2 HP Secs. 1344, 1345 (authority to censure disorderly member).

3. He shall decide all points of order, subject to an appeal by any member to the membership. On appeal, no member shall speak more than once unless by permission of a majority of the members present. See Rule I Clause 4, House Rules; see also 5 HP Sec. 6865 (requirement that question of order be presented in writing); 6 CP Sec. 249 (no duty to decide hypothetical questions); 4 HP Sec. 4637 (reversal of Presiding Officer's decisions); 5 HP Sec. 6002 (right of appeal); 8 CP Secs. 3453-55 (appeal as debatable).

4. He shall rise to put a question, but may state it sitting; and shall put questions in this form, to wit: "As many as are in favor, say 'Aye' "; and after the affirmative voice is expressed, "As many as are opposed, say 'No' "; if he doubts, or a division is called for, the members shall divide; those in

---

[1]Hereinafter cited as HP.

[2]Hereinafter cited as CP.

the affirmative of the question shall first rise from their seats and be counted by the Presiding Officer, and then those in the negative; if he still doubts, or a count is required by at least one fifth of a quorum, he shall name one or more from each side of the question to count the members in the affirmative and then those in the negative; the count being reported, he shall rise and state the decision. See Rule I Clause 6, House Rules; see also 6 CP Sec. 247 (motion as stated by the Presiding Officer as the proposition voted on); 5 HP Sec. 6002 (presumption of an honest count by Presiding Officer); 5 HP Sec. 5991 (taking vote again in case of doubt as to count by tellers).

5. He shall not be required to vote except where his vote would be decisive or where voting is by ballot. In case of a tie vote the question shall be lost. Rule I Clause 6, House Rules; 8 CP Sec. 3100 (authority of Presiding Officer to vote to make a tie or to vote to break a tie); 5 HP Sec. 5971 (withdrawal of Presiding Officer's vote where it was unnecessary).

6. He shall have the right to name any member to perform the duties of the chair, but such substitution shall not extend beyond three days. However, in case of his illness, he may make such appointment for a period not exceeding ten days, with the approval of the membership at the time such appointment is made; and in his absence and omission to make such appointment, the membership shall proceed to elect a Presiding Officer pro tempore to act during his absence. See Rule I Clause 7, House Rules; see also 2 HP Sec. 1405 (right of Members to elect a Presiding Officer pro tempore); 2 HP Sec. 1378 (designation of Presiding Officer pro tempore in writing).

RULE II. ELECTION OF OFFICERS

There shall be elected by a *viva voce* vote, at the commencement of each annual meeting, to continue in office until their successors are chosen and qualified, a Vice-president, a Treasurer, a Recording Secretary, a Sergeant at Arms, a Doorkeeper, and a Chaplain. Rule I, House Rules; elections generally, see 1 HP Ch. 6; 6 CP Ch. 153; see also 1 HP Sec. 204 (election of officer on a roll call); 1 HP Secs. 193, 194 (selection of officers by resolution); 6 CP Sec. 23 (majority vote as required for election of officers).

RULE III. DUTIES OF THE RECORDING SECRETARY

1. The Secretary shall, at the commencement of the annual meeting, call the members to order, proceed to call the roll of members, and, pending the election of the Presiding Officer or Chairman pro tempore, preserve order and decide all questions of procedure subject to appeal by any member. Rule III Clause 1, House Rules; see also 1 HP Sec. 84 (call of roll as not subject to interruption); 1 HP Secs. 19-24 (privilege of motion to proceed to election).

2. He shall record all questions of procedure, with the decisions thereon, in the minutes. He shall complete, as soon as possible after the close of the annual meeting, the printing and distribution of the minutes. He shall retain for the use of the members and officers one copy of all reports and official correspondence deposited with him. He shall record the passage of all resolutions, keep full and accurate accounts of the organization's disbursements, and pay to the organization's officers and employees the amount of their salaries that shall be due them. Rule III Clause 3, House Rules; see also 5 HP Sec. 7322 (duty of Clerk to furnish supplies to committees).

3. He shall, in case of temporary absence or disability, designate another officer to sign all papers that may require the official signature of the Secretary and to do all other acts that may be required of him under the rules and practice of this organization. Such official acts, when so done by the designated officer, shall be under the name of the Recording Secretary. The said designation shall be in writing and shall be laid before the membership and entered in the minutes. See Rule III Clause 4, House Rules; see also 6 CP Sec. 26 (form of designation of Clerk pro tempore).

RULE IV. DUTIES OF THE SERGEANT AT ARMS

It shall be the duty of the Sergeant at Arms to maintain order under the direction of the Presiding Officer, and, pending the election of a Presiding Officer, execute the instructions of the acting Presiding Officer. See Rule IV Clause 1, House Rules; see also 6 CP Sec. 37 (removal of Sergeant at Arms by resolution).

RULE V. DUTIES OF THE DOORKEEPER

1. The Doorkeeper shall enforce strictly the rules relating to the privileges of the floor and to the attendance or presence of members or other persons at meetings. See Rule V Clause 1, House Rules; See also 1 HP Sec. 262 (administrative duties of Doorkeeper).

2. He shall allow no unauthorized person to enter the meeting rooms during sittings; and fifteen minutes before the hour of meeting each day he shall see that the floor is cleared of all persons except those privileged to remain, and kept so until ten minutes after adjournment. See Rule V Clause 2, House Rules; see also 5 HP Sec. 6591 (announcements at the door).

RULE VI. DUTIES OF THE CHAPLAIN

The Chaplain shall attend at the commencement of each day's sitting and open the same with prayer. See Rule III, House Rules; see also 6 CP Sec. 663 (prayer as not requiring the presence of a quorum).

RULE VII. THE MEMBERS

1. Every member shall be present during sittings at the annual meeting, unless excused or necessarily prevented, and shall vote on each question put, unless he has a direct personal or pecuniary interest in the event of such question. Rule III Clause 1, House Rules; as to members generally, see 2 HP Ch. 41. See also 5 HP Secs. 5942-48 (impracticality of enforcing provisions requiring members to vote); 5 HP Secs. 5966, 5967 (right of members to vote as inherent); 5 HP Secs. 5955, 5958 (personal interest as disqualifying); 8 CP Sec. 3074 (personal interest as basis for resignation from a committee).

RULE VIII. QUESTIONS OF PRIVILEGE

1. Questions of privilege shall be, first, those affecting the rights of the membership collectively, its safety, dignity, and the integrity of its proceedings; second, the rights, reputation, and conduct of members individually, in their capacity as members only. See Rule IX, House Rules; privilege of

House or member generally, see 3 HP Chs. 81, 82, and 6 CP
Chs. 204, 205. See also 3 HP Secs. 2645-47 (conduct of offi-
cers and employees as raising question of privilege); 7 CP
Sec. 911 (newspaper charges as raising question of privilege).

2. Questions of privilege shall have precedence over all
other questions, except motions to adjourn. See Rule IX,
House Rules; see also 3 HP Sec. 2522 (precedents of questions of privilege); 8 CP Sec. 2448 (debate on question of
privilege).

RULE IX. STANDING COMMITTEES

1. Standing committees shall be appointed by the Presiding Officer at the commencement of each Annual Meeting. See Rule X Clause 1, House Rules; committees generally, see 4 HP Chs. 99-106 and 7 CP Chs. 228-33; see also 8
CP Sec. 2171 (election of committees by motion or resolution
from the floor); 8 CP Sec. 2179 (motion as privileged).

2. The Presiding Officer shall appoint all select committees that shall be created by the membership from time to
time. See Rule X Clause 2, House Rules; see also 4 HP Secs.
4448, 4470 (inherent authority of Presiding Officer to appoint
a select committee); 4 HP Secs. 4517-23 (considerations involved in appointing member moving a select committee as
its chairman).

3. In the temporary absence of the chairman the
member next in rank shall act as chairman; and in case of a
permanent vacancy in the chairmanship, he shall be selected
in the same manner as the original chairman shall have been
selected. See Rule X Clause 4, House Rules; 4 HP Sec. 4669
(ordering report to be made by chairman or committee
member); 4 HP Sec. 4424 (first-named member to act as
chairman).

RULE X. POWERS AND DUTIES OF COMMITTEES

1. All proposed resolutions, petitions, and other matters relating to the subjects listed under the standing committees named below shall be referred to such committees,
respectively:

    a.   *Committee on Operations* (see Rule XI Clause
8, House Rules).

(1) Evaluating budget and accounting measures; costs of operations.

(2) Studying the operation of this organization's activities at all levels with a view to determining its economy and efficiency.

(3) Evaluating the scope and effect of services to members.

b. *Committee on Administration* (see Rule XI Clause 9, House Rules).

(1) Auditing and settling of all accounts.

(2) Measures relating to the employment of persons by this organization; health insurance and other employee benefits.

(3) Measures relating to assignment of office space.

(4) Measures relating to the disposition of useless papers.

(5) Measures relating to the election of the officers; contested elections; credentials and qualifications.

(6) Measures relating to the travel of officers, members, and employees.

c. *Committee on Rules* (see Rule XI Clause 17, House Rules).

(1) Standing rules.

(2) Order of business.

(3) Changes in rules and bylaws.

2. a. Each standing or select committee shall fix, by written rule adopted by the committee, regular meeting days for the conduct of its business. Each such committee shall meet, for the consideration of any matter pending before the committee or for the transaction of other committee business, on all regular meeting days fixed by the committee, unless otherwise provided by written rule adopted by the committee. See Rule XI Clause 26, House Rules; 8 CP Secs. 2213, 2214 (authority to transact business in the absence of the chairman).

b. The chairman of each standing or select committee may call and convene, as he considers necessary, additional meetings of the committee for the consideration of any matter pending before the committee or for the consideration of other committee business. The committee shall meet for such purpose pursuant to the call of the chairman. See Rule XI Clause 26, House Rules; 8 CP Sec. 2213 (calling meetings without the consent of the chairman).

c. If at least three members of any standing or select committee desire that a special meeting of the committee be called by the chairman, those members may file with the chairman their written request for that special meeting. Such request shall specify the measure or matter to be considered. If, within three calendar days after the filing of the request, the chairman does not call the requested special meeting, a majority of the members of the committee may issue their written notice to all members that a special meeting of the committee will be held, specifying the place, date, and hour of, and the measure or matter to be considered at, that special meeting. The committee shall meet on that date and at that hour. Only the measure or matter specified in that notice may be considered at that special meeting. See Rule XI Clause 26, House Rules; 8 CP Sec. 2208.

d. If the chairman of any standing committee is not present at any regular, additional, or special meeting of the committee, the ranking member on the committee who is present shall preside at that meeting. See Rule XI Clause 26, House Rules.

3. a. The rules of this organization are the rules of its committees and subcommittees so far as applicable, except that a motion to recess from day to day is a motion of high privilege in committees and subcommittees. Each committee may adopt written rules not inconsistent with the rules of this

organization, and those rules shall be binding on each subcommittee of that committee. Each subcommittee of a committee is a part of that committee and is subject to the authority and direction of that committee. See Rule XI Clause 27, House Rules; 3 HP Secs. 1841, 1842 (adoption of committee rules); 6 CP Sec. 532 (appointment of subcommittees).

b.   Each committee shall keep complete minutes. Such minutes shall include a record of the votes on any question on which a record vote has been taken. With respect to each record vote by any committee on each motion to report any matter, the total number of votes cast for, and the total number of votes cast against, the reporting of such matter shall be included in the committee report. See Rule XI Clause 27, House Rules.

c.   (1)   It shall be the duty of the chairman of each committee to report promptly to the full membership any measure approved by the committee and to take necessary steps to bring the matter before the assembly. See Rule XI Clause 27, House Rules.

    (2)   If, at the time of approval of any measure or matter by any committee, any member of the committee desires to file supplemental, minority, or additional views, that member shall be entitled to file such views in writing and signed by that member, with the committee. All such views so filed by one or more members of the committee shall be included within, and shall be a part of, the report filed by the committee with respect to that measure or matter. See Rule XI Clause 27, House Rules.

d.   No measure or recommendation shall be reported from any committee unless a majority of the committee were actually present. No vote by any member of any committee with respect to any measure or matter may be cast by proxy unless such committee, by written rule adopted by the committee, permits voting by proxy and requires that the proxy authorization shall be in writing, shall designate the person who is to execute the proxy authorization, and shall be limited to a specific measure or matter and any amendments or motions pertaining thereto. See Rule XI Clause 27, House Rules.

e.   No point of order shall lie with respect to any measure reported by any committee on the ground that hearings upon such measure were not conducted in accordance with the provisions of this clause unless such point of order was timely made in committee. See Rule XI Clause 27, House Rules.

4. Each committee may fix the number of its members to constitute a quorum for a hearing, which shall be not less than two. See Rule XI Clause 27, House Rules; see also *Christoffel* v. *U.S.*, 338 U.S. 84, observing that a committee is not a "competent tribunal" during a period when less than a quorum of the committee is in attendance.

RULE XI. CALENDARS AND REPORTS OF COMMITTEES

1. There shall be a calendar to which all business reported from committees shall be referred. See Rule XIII Clause 1, House Rules; 4 HP Sec. 3117 (matters improperly reported as not entitled to a place on the calendar); 7 CP Sec. 859 (authority of Presiding Officer to change calendar reference).

2. All reports of committees, together with the views of the minority, shall be delivered to the Secretary for reference to the calendar under the direction of the Presiding Officer. However, matters reported adversely shall be laid on the table, unless the committee reporting a matter, at the time, or any member within three days thereafter, shall request its reference to the calendar, when it shall be referred, as provided above. See Rule XIII Clause 2, House Rules; 4 HP Sec. 4600 (presentation of minority views not filed with the consent of the membership).

3. The report accompanying each resolution reported by any committee shall contain an estimate, made by such committee, of the costs that would be incurred in carrying out such resolution in the fiscal year in which it is reported and in each of the five fiscal years following such fiscal year (or for the authorized duration of any program authorized by such, if less than five years). See Rule XIII Clause 7, House Rules.

RULE XII. DECORUM AND DEBATE

1. When any member desires to speak, he shall rise and respectfully address himself to "Mr. Chairman [or Madam Chairman]," or whatever the Presiding Officer's title may be, and, on being recognized, may address the membership; he shall confine himself to the question under debate, avoiding personality. See Rule XIV Clause 1, House Rules; debate generally, see 5 HP Chs. 112-16; see also 5 HP Secs. 4982-85 (necessity that motion be made and stated or read before proceeding to debate); 8 CP Secs. 2455-58 (parliamentary inquiries as not depriving member of the floor); 8 CP Sec. 2476 (effect of yielding to another member to offer an amendment as losing the floor); 5 HP Secs. 5043-48 (strictly confining member to subject under debate).

2. When two or more members rise at once, the Presiding Officer shall name the member who is first to speak; and no member shall occupy more than one hour in debate on any question except as further provided in this rule. See Rule XIV Clause 2, House Rules; 2 HP Sec. 1424 (discretion of Presiding Officer in recognizing a member); 2 HP Sec. 1447 (priority in recognizing member who represents reporting committee); 6 CP Secs. 302-5 (moving member as entitled to prior recognition).

3. The member reporting the measure under consideration from a committee may open and close, where general debate has been had thereon; and if it shall extend beyond one day, he shall be entitled to one hour to close, notwithstanding he may have used an hour in opening. See Rule XIV Clause 3, House Rules; 5 HP Secs. 4997-5000 (ordering of previous question as limiting right to close).

4. If any member, in speaking or otherwise, transgress the rules of this organization, the Presiding Officer shall, or any member may, call him to order; in which case he shall

immediately sit down, unless permitted, on motion of
another member, to explain, and the membership shall, if
appealed to, decide the case without debate; if the decision is
in favor of the member called to order, he shall be at liberty
to proceed, but not otherwise; and, if the case requires it, he
shall be liable to censure or such punishment as the membership may deem proper. See Rule XIV Clause 4, House
Rules; 5 HP Sec. 5187 (precedence of motion that member
be permitted to explain); 5 HP Secs. 5196-99 (member held
out of order as losing the floor).

5. If a member is called to order for words spoken in
debate, the member calling him to order shall indicate the
words excepted to, and they shall be taken down in writing
by the Secretary and read aloud to the membership; but he
shall not be held to answer, nor be subject to censure therefor, if further debate or other business has intervened. Rule
XIV Clause 5, House Rules; 5 HP Sec. 6944 (decision of
Presiding Officer as to whether words are in order as final).

6. No member shall speak more than once to the same
question without leave of the membership, unless he be the
mover, proposer, or introducer of the matter pending, in
which case he shall be permitted to speak in reply, but not
until every member choosing to speak shall have spoken. See
Rule XIV Clause 6, House Rules; 5 HP Secs. 4993, 4994
(right to speak to an amendment after having spoken once to
the main question); 5 HP Sec. 4992 (timeliness of point of
order that a member has spoken already).

7. While the Presiding Officer is putting a question or
addressing the membership, no member shall leave the
meeting, nor, when a member is speaking, pass between him
and the chair. See Rule XIV Clause 7, House Rules.

RULE XIII. CALLS OF THE ROLL

1. On every roll call the names of the members shall be
called alphabetically by surname, except when two or more
have the same surname, in which case the whole name shall
be called, and after the roll has been once called, the Secretary shall call in their alphabetical order the names of those
not voting. Members appearing after the second call, but
before the result is announced, may vote. Rule XV Clause 1,
House Rules; 8 CP Sec. 3162 (motion for correction of Journal); 8 CP Sec. 3126 (motion that vote be recapitulated); 5

HP Secs. 5931-33 (right of member to change his vote before announcement of result); 5 HP Sec. 5930 (right of member to withdraw vote).

2. On the demand of any member, or at the suggestion of the Presiding Officer, the names of members sufficient to make a quorum who are present but do not vote shall be noted by the Secretary and be counted and announced in determining the presence of a quorum to do business. See Rule XV Clause 3, House Rules; 8 CP Sec. 3152.

3. Whenever a quorum fails to vote on any question, and a quorum is not present and objection is made for that cause, unless the membership shall adjourn there shall be a call of the members, and the yeas and nays on the pending question shall at the same time be considered as ordered. The Secretary shall call the roll, and each member as he answers to his name may vote on the pending question. If those voting on the question and those who are present and decline to vote shall together make a majority, the Presiding Officer shall declare that a quorum is constituted and announce the vote on the pending question; thereupon, further proceedings under the call shall be considered as dispensed with. If a quorum does not appear at any time after the roll call has been completed, the Presiding Officer may entertain a motion to adjourn, if seconded by a majority of those present, to be ascertained by actual count; and if the membership adjourns, all proceedings under this section shall be vacated. See Rule XV Clause 4, House Rules; 4 HP Secs. 2994, 3029 (motions that may be agreed to by less than a quorum); 4 HP Sec. 3050 (motions to adjourn before the call begins). Adoption and use of electronic voting devices, see Rule XV Clause 5, House Rules.

RULE XIV. MOTIONS

1. Every proper motion shall be reduced to writing on the demand of any member, and shall be entered on the minutes with the name of the member making it, unless it is withdrawn the same day. See Rule XVI Clause 1, House Rules; motions generally, see 5 HP Ch. 117 and 8 CP Ch. 247; 4 HP Secs. 2844-46 (motions not entertained are not entered on the minutes).

2. When a motion has been made, the Presiding Officer shall state it or (if it is in writing) cause it to be read aloud

before being debated; such a motion may be withdrawn at any time before a decision or an amendment has been agreed to. See Rule XVI Clause 2, House Rules; 5 HP Sec. 5304 (practice of requiring a second for every motion as obsolete); 8 CP Sec. 2332 (withdrawal of amendment before decision thereon).

3. When any motion or proposition is made, the question "Will the membership now consider it?" shall not be put unless demanded by a member; if put, it shall be decided without debate. See Rule XVI Clause 3, House Rules; 5 HP Sec. 4940 (refusal to consider as not amounting to rejection of a matter); 8 CP Sec. 2447 (question of consideration as not debatable); 5 HP Secs. 4937-39 (timeliness of demand for the question of consideration after debate has begun).

4. When a question is under debate, no motion shall be received but to adjourn, to lay on the table, for the previous question (which motions shall be decided without debate), to postpone to a day certain, to refer, amend, or postpone indefinitely; such motions shall have precedence in the foregoing order. No motion to postpone to a day certain, to refer, or to postpone indefinitely, being decided, shall be again allowed on the same day at the same stage of the question. After the previous question shall have been ordered on the passage of a resolution, one motion to recommit shall be in order, and the Presiding Officer shall give preference in recognition for such purpose to a member who is opposed to the resolution. However, with respect to any motion to recommit with instructions after the previous question shall have been ordered, it always shall be in order to debate such motion for ten minutes before the vote is taken on that motion. One half of such time may be allotted to the mover of the motion and one half to the member in opposition to the motion. It shall be in order at any time during a day for the Presiding Officer, in his discretion, to entertain a motion that when the membership adjourns it stand adjourned to a day and time certain. Such a motion shall be of equal privilege with the motion to adjourn provided for in this clause and shall be determined without debate. See Rule XVI Clause 4, House Rules; 3 HP Sec. 2521 (precedence of motion to adjourn); 8 CP Sec. 2647 (motion to adjourn as in order in simple form only); 5 HP Sec. 5359 (motion to adjourn as not debatable); 5 HP Sec. 5389 (motion to table as final, adverse disposition of matter without debate); 5 HP Sec. 5054 (motion to refer as debatable).

5. The hour at which the membership adjourns shall be entered on the minutes. See Rule XVI Clause 5, House Rules; 5 HP Sec. 6740.

6. On the demand of any member, before the question is put, a question shall be divided if it includes propositions so distinct in substance that, one being taken away, a substantive proposition shall remain, provided that any motion or resolution to elect the members or any portion of the members of the standing committees shall not be divisible. Rule XVI Clause 6, House Rules; 5 HP Sec. 6162 (limitation on dividing a question after it has been put); 5 HP Secs. 6108-13 (requirement of two substantive propositions in order to justify division); 5 HP Sec. 5468 (permissibility of dividing a matter after the previous question is ordered).

7. A motion to strike out and insert is indivisible, but a motion to strike out being lost shall neither preclude amendment nor motion to strike out and insert. Rule XVI Clause 7, House Rules.

8. No motion or proposition on a subject different from that under consideration shall be admitted under color of amendment. See Rule XVI Clause 7, House Rules; 5 HP Ch. 126 (general rule that amendment should be germane to the particular paragraph or section to which offered); 8 CP Sec. 2911 (requirement that purpose of amendment be germane to purpose of proposition to which it is offered); 5 HP Sec. 5806 (germaneness rule as applicable to amendments reported by committees).

9. Pending a motion to suspend the rules, the Presiding Officer may entertain one motion that the membership adjourn; but after the result thereon is announced he shall not entertain any other motion until the vote is taken on the motion to suspend. See Rule XVI Clause 8, House Rules; 5 HP Secs. 5744-46 (second motion to adjourn after a quorum has failed).

10. No dilatory motion shall be entertained by the Presiding Officer. Rule XVI Clause 10, House Rules; 5 HP Secs. 5731-33 (motions to adjourn as dilatory); 8 CP Sec. 2797 (motion to reconsider as dilatory); 8 CP Sec. 2816 (motion to table as dilatory).

Rule XV. Previous Question

1. There shall be a motion for the previous question, which, being ordered by a majority of members voting with a

quorum present, shall terminate all debate and bring the membership to a direct vote upon the immediate question or questions on which it has been asked and ordered. The previous question may be asked and ordered upon a single motion, a series of motions allowable under the rules, or an amendment or amendments, or may be made to embrace all authorized motions or amendments and include the resolution to its passage or rejection. It shall be in order, pending such motion, or after the previous question shall have been ordered on its passage, for the Presiding Officer to entertain and submit one motion to commit, with or without instructions, to a standing or select committee. Rule XVI Clause 4 and Rule XVII Clause 1, House Rules; 5 HP Sec. 5456 (motion for previous question as closing debate); 2 HP Sec. 1256 (motion as applicable to questions of privilege); 8 CP Sec. 3433 (motion for previous question as not in order when point of order is pending). Moving the previous question generally, see 5 HP Ch. 120 and 8 CP Ch. 250.

2. A call of the membership shall not be in order after the previous question is ordered, unless it shall appear upon an actual count by the Presiding Officer that a quorum is not present. Rule XVII Clause 2, House Rules.

3. All incidental questions of order arising after a motion is made for the previous question, and pending such motion, shall be decided, whether on appeal or otherwise, without debate. Rule XVII Clause 3, House Rules; 5 HP Sec. 5448 (purpose of rule as preventing delay by debate on points of order after the demand of the previous question).

Rule XVI. Reconsideration

1. When a motion has been made and carried or lost, it shall be in order for any member of the majority, on the same or the succeeding day, to move for the reconsideration thereof, and such motion shall take precedence over all other questions except a motion to adjourn, and shall not be withdrawn after the said succeeding day without the consent of the membership; and thereafter any member may call it up for consideration. Rule XVIII Clause 1, House Rules; 5 HP Sec. 5605 (motion to reconsider as used in the Continental Congress); 5 HP Sec. 5606 (motion to reconsider as not in order in absence of quorum).

2. No resolution referred to a committee shall be

brought back before the membership on a motion to reconsider; all resolutions reported from a committee shall be accompanied by reports in writing. See Rule XVIII Clause 2, House Rules; 5 HP Sec. 5647 (purpose of rule as preventing use of motion to bring before the membership matters otherwise not in order).

RULE XVII. AMENDMENTS

When a motion or proposition is under consideration, a motion to amend and a motion to amend that amendment shall be in order. It shall also be in order to offer a further amendment by way of substitute, to which one amendment may be offered, but which shall not be voted on until the original matter is perfected, but either may be withdrawn before amendment or decision is had thereon. Amendments to the title of a resolution shall not be in order until after its passage and shall be decided without debate. Rule XIX, House Rules; amendments generally, see 5 HP Ch. 125 and 8 CP Ch. 255; 8 CP Secs. 2883, 2887 (permissibility of the four motions specified as pending at one and the same time); 8 CP Sec. 2888 (amendments in the third degree as not permissible); 5 HP Sec. 5773 (priority of amendments reported by committee before those offered from floor).

RULE XVIII. RESOLUTIONS

All resolutions may be delivered, endorsed with the names of members introducing them, to the Presiding Officer, to be by him referred; and resolutions and related documents so referred shall be entered on the minutes. Correction in case of error of reference may be made by the membership without debate on any day immediately after the approval of the minutes, by unanimous consent, or on motion of a committee claiming jurisdiction, or on the report of the committee to which the subject has been erroneously referred. Rule XXII Clause 4, House Rules; 7 CP Sec. 2124 (precedence of motion for change of reference); 7 CP Secs. 2126-28 (motion for change of reference as not debatable); 7 CP Sec. 2110 (timeliness of motion for change of reference after committee action).

RULE XIX. COMMITTEES OF THE WHOLE

1. In all cases, in forming a committee of the whole, the Presiding Officer shall leave the chair after appointing a chairman to preside, who shall, in case of disturbance or disorderly conduct in the hall, have power to cause the same to be cleared. See Rule XXIII Clause 1, House Rules; 5 HP Sec. 6987 (authority of Presiding Officer to direct exclusion of disorderly words).

2. Whenever a committee of the whole finds itself without a quorum, which shall consist of one half of the general quorum requirement for the organization, the chairman shall invoke the procedure for the call of the roll. See Rule XXIII Clause 2, House Rules; 4 HP Secs. 2975-76 (quorum as unnecessary for motion that committee of the whole rise).

3. In committees of the whole, business on their calendars may be taken up in regular order, or in such order as the committee may determine, unless the subject to be considered was determined by the membership at the time of going into committee. See Rule XXIII Clause 4, House Rules; 4 CP Sec. 4730 (motion to establish an order of consideration of matters); 8 CP Sec. 2333 (motion to take up matter out of its order).

4. When general debate is closed by order of the membership, any member shall be allowed five minutes to explain any amendment he may offer, after which the member who shall first obtain the floor shall be allowed to speak five minutes in opposition to it, and there shall be no further debate thereon, but the same privilege of debate shall be allowed against any amendment that may be offered to an amendment; and neither an amendment nor an amendment to an amendment shall be withdrawn by the mover thereof unless by the unanimous consent of the committee. See Rule XXIII Clause 5, House Rules; 5 HP Sec. 5208 (time for motion to close general debate in committee of the whole).

5. The committee may, by the vote of a majority of the members present, at any time after the five minutes' debate has begun upon proposed amendments to any section or paragraph, close all debate upon such section or paragraph, or, at its election, upon the pending amendments only (which motion shall be decided without debate); but this shall not preclude further amendment, to be decided without debate. See Rule XXIII Clause 6, House Rules; 5 HP

Sec. 5227 (motion to close debate as subject to amendment); 5 HP Sec. 5734 (motion to close debate as dilatory).

6. The procedural Rules of Order of this organization shall be observed in committees of the whole so far as they may be applicable. See Rule XXIII Clause 8, House Rules.

RULE XX. ORDER OF BUSINESS

1. The daily order of business shall be as follows:

First.   Prayer by the Chaplain.
Second.   Reading and approval of the minutes.
Third.   Correction of reference of resolutions.
Fourth.   Disposal of business on the Presiding Officer's table.
Fifth.   Unfinished business.
Sixth.   Motions to go into Committee of the Whole.
Seventh. New business and orders of the day.
Eighth.   Motions to discharge a committee.

See Rule XXIV Clause 1, House Rules; 4 HP Secs. 3070, 3071 (business interrupted by privileged matter as going on from place of interruption).

2. The consideration of the unfinished business in which the membership may be engaged at an adjournment shall be resumed as soon as the business on the Presiding Officer's table is finished, and the consideration of all other unfinished business shall be resumed whenever the class of business to which it belongs shall be in order under the rules. Rule XXIV Clause 3, House Rules.

3. After the unfinished business has been disposed of, the Presiding Officer shall then call each standing committee in regular order, and then select committees, and each committee when named may call up for consideration any resolution reported by it, and if he shall not complete the call of the committees before the membership passes to other business, he shall resume the next call where he left off, giving preference to the last matter under consideration.

RULE XXI. PRIORITY OF BUSINESS

All questions relating to the priority of business shall be decided by a majority without debate. See Rule XXV, House

Rules; 5 HP Sec. 6952 (appeal from decision of the Presiding Officer as to the priority of business as not debatable).

RULE XXII. CHANGE OR SUSPENSION OF RULES

1. No rule shall be suspended except by a vote of two thirds of the members voting, a quorum being present. Rule XXVII Clause 1, House Rules; 5 HP Secs. 6852, 6853 (use of motion to suspend rule for the order of business to permit consideration of a particular matter); 5 HP Sec. 5752 (motion as suspending all rules inconsistent with its purposes); 5 HP Sec. 6825 (motion to suspend the rules and consider another matter is not in order when question of high privilege is pending).

2. All motions to suspend the rules shall, before being submitted to the membership, be seconded by a majority by tellers, if demanded. See Rule XXVII Clause 2, House Rules; 5 HP Sec. 6800 (practice of Presiding Officer to ask, "Is a second demanded?"); 8 CP Sec. 3405 (withdrawal of motion); 5 HP Sec. 6840 (modification of motion may be made prior to the second being ordered).

3. When a motion to suspend the rules has been seconded, it shall be in order, before the final vote is taken thereon, to debate the motion for forty minutes, one half of such time to be given to debate in favor of the motion and one half to debate in opposition thereto. The same right of debate shall be allowed whenever the previous question has been ordered on any proposition on which there has been no debate. See Rule XXVII Clause 3, House Rules; 5 HP Secs. 6823, 6824 (division of time for debate between mover and seconder).

RULE XXIII. MOTIONS TO DISCHARGE

1. Any member may move to discharge a committee from the consideration of a proposition that has been referred to it thirty days prior thereto. See Rule XVII Clause 4, House Rules.

2. The membership shall proceed to the consideration of a motion to discharge without intervening motion except one motion to adjourn. After twenty minutes' debate, one half in favor of the motion to discharge and one half in opposition thereto, the membership shall proceed to vote on such motion. If the motion prevails, it shall then be in order for

any member to move that the membership proceed to the
immediate consideration of the referred proposition (such
motion not being debatable), and if it shall be decided in the
affirmative, the matter shall be immediately considered.
Should the membership by vote decide against the immediate consideration of such proposition, it shall be rere-
ferred to the committee to which it was originally referred.
See Rule XXVII Clause 4, House Rules; 7 CP Sec. 1010a
(right to close debate on motion reserved to proponents
thereof).

RULE XXIV. SECRET SESSIONS

Whenever the Presiding Officer or any member shall
inform the membership that he has communications that he
believes ought to be kept secret for the present, the meeting
shall be cleared of all persons except members and officers
during the reading of such communications and during the
debates and proceedings thereon, unless otherwise ordered
by the membership. See Rule XXIV, House Rules; 5 HP
Sec. 7254 (motions to remove the injunction of secrecy behind closed doors).

RULE XXV. READING OF PAPERS

When the reading of a paper other than one upon which
the membership is called to give a final vote is demanded,
and the same is objected to by any member, it shall be
determined without debate by a vote of the members. See
Rule XXX, House Rules; 5 HP Sec. 5258 (right of member to
read paper on which membership is to vote); 6 CP Sec. 606,
8 CP Sec. 2599 (right to read paper involving a matter of
privilege).

RULE XXVI. PAPERS

The several committees shall, within three days after
the final adjournment of the annual meeting, deliver to the
Recording Secretary all papers referred to the committee,
together with all evidence taken by such committee during
the preceding year and not reported to the membership; and
in the event of the failure or neglect of any committee to
comply with this rule the Recording Secretary shall, within

three days thereafter, take into his keeping all such papers
and evidence. See Rule XXXVI, House Rules.

RULE XXVII. BALLOTS

In all cases of ballot a majority of the votes given shall be
necessary to an election, and where there shall not be such a
majority on the first ballot, the ballots shall be repeated until
a majority be obtained; and in all balloting, blanks shall be
rejected and not taken into the count in enumeration of votes
or reported by the tellers. See Rule XXXVIII, House Rules.

RULE XXVIII. FORMS

Putting the Questions

The forms of putting ordinary questions are:
The Presiding Officer, rising, says: "As many as are in
favor say 'Aye.' "
And after the affirmative voice is expressed: "As many as
are opposed say 'No.' "
If a division is demanded, the Presiding Officer says: "As
many as are in favor will rise and stand until counted."
And after the count of the affirmative: "The ayes will be
seated and the noes will stand."
If tellers are ordered: "The gentleman from [DISTRICT],
Mr. [NAME], and the gentleman from [DISTRICT], Mr. [NAME],
will take their places as tellers. As many as are in favor will
now pass between the tellers and be counted."
After those in the affirmative have been counted the
tellers report the number to the chair; after which the chair
announces: "As many as are opposed will now pass between
the tellers and be counted."
The number of those in the negative is reported, after
which there is an opportunity for additional members to vote
on either side, the tellers reporting the additions. (Tellers
should be on the alert to prevent any member from voting
twice.) Then the Chair reports the vote.
Form for putting the previous question: "The gentleman
from [DISTRICT] moves the previous question. As many as are
in favor of ordering the previous question will say 'Aye'; as
many as are opposed will say 'No.' "

Orders and Resolutions

Form of an order:
> *Ordered,* That the hour of daily meeting of this organization shall be 12 M.

Form of simple resolution:
> *Resolved,* That the membership declines to consider any matter that involves an expenditure of money for political purposes.

Form of resolution for adjournment *sine die*:
> *Resolved,* That the Assembly shall adjourn on [DAY], December [DATE, YEAR], and that when they adjourn on said day, they stand adjourned *sine die.*

Form of resolution for a recess:
> *Resolved,* That when the members recess on [DAY, MONTH, DATE, YEAR], they stand in recess until 12 o'clock meridian, [DAY, MONTH, DATE, YEAR].

Form of Report From Committee of the Whole

The Committee of the Whole having risen, the Presiding Officer says: "The Committee of the Whole having had under consideration the resolution [NUMBER AND TITLE] directs me to report the same with amendments, with the recommendation that [*the amendments be agreed to and that*] the resolution do pass."

If there are no amendments, or if several resolutions are reported at once, or if the Committee of the Whole recommends that a resolution do not pass or be laid on the table, the report is modified accordingly.

If the Committee of the Whole has not concluded consideration; the chairman reports that "the committee has come to no resolution thereon."

Form of Report From Standing or Select Committee

The Committee on [NAME OF COMMITTEE] to whom was referred the resolution "to provide," etc., having considered the same, report it [*with amendments specified*] with the recommendation that the amendments be agreed to and that the resolution as so amended do pass [*or do not pass, or be laid on the table, etc.*].

Resolution Providing for an Investigation

Resolved, That a select committee of five members be appointed by the Presiding Officer to investigate and report not later than [DATE], with respect to the following matters: . . .

—7—

OFFICERS AND EMPLOYEES

Sec. 45. Kinds of Officers

The officers of a membership organization are generally of two types—elective and appointive. Both should be identified in the bylaws, and their respective duties should be carefully defined. In general, the elective officers are given policy-making responsibilities, whereas appointed officers are given executive and administrative duties.

In creating elective offices, many membership organizations have followed the practice of the U.S. House of Representatives. In the House the elective officers are, in addition to the Speaker, a Clerk, Sergeant at Arms, Doorkeeper, Postmaster, and Chaplain. (Rule II, House Rules.)

Although they do not, of course, have postmasters or chaplains, most membership organizations have other comparable elected officers, such as a president or chairman, a clerk or recording officer, a treasurer, and sometimes a sergeant at arms and doorkeeper. Most membership organizations also have a board of directors, and this, too, is an elective body. (Election procedures are discussed elsewhere in this work; see Secs. 59-75.)

It should not be assumed that these officers are somehow supreme in their authority over the affairs of the organization. The relationship between the members and the organization, as represented by its elected officers and the board of directors, is unique. The member is the person served by the organization; he is also the ultimate source of power from which the various officers and the board of directors derive their authority. Therefore, when a conflict of authority appears between two or more officers, the membership may appoint a select committee to investigate and report on the matter. (1 Hinds' Precedents[1] Sec. 250.)

[1]Hereinafter cited as HP.

Nor should it be assumed that the president or chairman routinely exercises control over the other elected officers of the organization. In fact, the chairman or president has no special authority over the other elected officials in the organization. It is the board of directors or the membership itself that should have control over the elected officers, and this may be provided for in the bylaws.

Sec. 46. Terms of Office

In most membership organizations the officers are elected for a term of one year. A relatively small number of membership organizations elect their officers for two- or three-year periods, and of this group most prefer the two-year period.

Most membership organizations allow officers to succeed themselves and do not place a limit on the number of terms an officer may serve, but a few prohibit an officer from succeeding himself, and some place a limit on the number of consecutive terms an officer may serve.

With respect to the length of the term of office, a distinction should be made between the presiding officer and the other officers of the organization. In the U.S. House of Representatives the term of office of the Speaker terminates with the end of the Congress for which he was elected, normally a two-year period. The other House officers, on the other hand, continue in a new Congress until their successors are chosen and qualified. (Rule II, House Rules Sec. 635; 1 HP Sec. 187.) This distinction is recognized in the bylaws of most membership organizations, thereby ensuring that the organization will not be left leaderless pending the election of new officers. Thus, when the membership decides to postpone the election of one of its officers, the officer from the prior annual or biannual session is deemed to continue in office until a successor is chosen. (1 HP Sec. 263.)

When an elected officer resigns, the membership may instruct another officer to perform the duties of the office until the beginning of the next session (1 HP Sec. 268) or annual meeting. And although, ordinarily, the election of an officer gives rise to a question of privilege (1 HP Sec. 273), a resolution transferring the duties of one officer of the organization to another does not involve the question of privilege. (1 HP Sec. 263.)

Sec. 47. Presiding Officer

The presiding officer or chairman is the chief elected officer in the great majority of membership organizations. Upon election (see Sec. 59 *infra*), he becomes the presiding officer at the meeting and has many other duties and responsibilities (see Secs. 88 *et seq. infra*). It is customary, after his election, for the presiding officer to address the membership, briefly or at length. The swearing in of the newly elected chairman, which may take place before or after his address, is performed by the member having the longest period of service in the organization. (1 HP Secs. 81, 220.)

A chairman pro tempore, to serve in the absence of the chairman, may be elected or appointed, depending upon the procedures specified in the bylaws. The bylaws should also indicate whether the chairman pro tempore is to have all of the powers of the chairman himself, including the power to sign documents and perform other duties devolving upon the chairman. (1 HP Sec. 229.)

If the office of chairman becomes vacant, as by his death or resignation, the organization should ordinarily proceed to the election of a new presiding officer. (See Sec. 59 *infra*). In such cases, the clerk presides until a successor is elected. (1 HP Sec. 231.) Thus, when the chairman resigns (1 HP Sec. 233) or dies (1 HP Sec. 234), it devolves upon the clerk to call the membership to order, ascertain the presence of a quorum, and entertain a motion to proceed to the election of a new chairman.

If the presiding officer finds that he must step down from his office, as where he finds that he is no longer in harmony with the majority of the membership, he may resign or recognize a member for a motion declaring his office vacant. (6 Cannon's Precedents[2] Sec. 35.) He may submit his resignation, to take effect upon the election of his successor, verbally. (1 HP Sec. 225.) Or he may submit his resignation by letter addressed to the membership, as follows:

> I respectfully ask [NAME OF ORGANIZATION] to allow me to resign the office of Presiding Officer, which I have the honor to hold, and to consider this as the act of my resignation. [1 HP Sec. 232.]

When the chairman resigns, no special action excusing him from service need be taken by the membership. (1 HP Sec. 232.)

[2]Hereinafter cited as CP.

Sec. 48. Clerk or Recording Secretary

The clerk or recording secretary may be elected or appointed, depending on the size of the organization and the functions of his office. As noted earlier, the office of chairman terminates with the expiration of the session or convention for which he was elected. (See Sec. 46 *supra*.) The clerk, on the other hand, should be deemed to continue in office until a successor is elected or appointed. This ensures continuity in the organizational structure and permits the clerk to preside while a new chairman is being nominated and elected. (1 HP Sec. 235.) If the bylaws do not provide for the continuation of the office of clerk, then a member may submit a resolution to that effect. This resolution may take the following form:

> *Resolved,* That the Clerk of [NAME OF ORGANIZATION] shall be deemed to continue in office until another be appointed [*or elected*]. [1 HP Sec. 235.]

In the event of his temporary absence or disability, the clerk may designate a clerk pro tempore. (6 CP Sec. 25.) The designation should be in writing and may take the following form, addressed to the presiding officer:

> Desiring to be temporarily absent from my office, I hereby designate [NAME OF MEMBER], an official in my office, to sign any and all papers for me which he would be authorized to sign by virtue of this designation and by the standing rules of this organization.
>
> Yours respectfully,

If the clerk or secretary dies during a period of recess or adjournment, the organization should be informed of this fact as soon as a quorum is ascertained and the members seated. It should then elect or appoint a successor at once, so as to prevent an interruption in the flow of its business. (1 HP Sec. 236.) A resolution to transact certain other business is out of order, because the filling of the vacancy in the office of the clerk is a matter of privilege, and because the membership would not be organized to do business until the vacancy is filled. (1 HP Sec. 237.)

Sec. 49. Duties of Office

It is the duty of an organization's clerk or secretary to keep a record of every official meeting. He should keep a record of all important events as they occur, including such matters as the election of directors and officers, policy decisions, bylaw changes, voting results, and the like.

The clerk is also, in many ways, a historian for the organization. One or more stenographers may be necessary to assist him in this regard. In more formal organizations, in fact, the proceedings are taken down verbatim so that they can be transcribed and printed at a later time.

His specific duties should be set forth in the bylaws (see Rule III, House Rules) and should include the following minimum responsibilities:

> 1.   Calls the roll of members at the inception of a new session or meeting and, pending the election of a chairman, preserves order and decides questions of procedure.
>
> 2.   Prepares and makes available to members a list of reports to be submitted by the officers of the organization.
>
> 3.   Makes a record of meetings and of questions of order or procedure that arise, with decisions thereon, to be kept in the form of minutes.
>
> 4.   Makes or approves all contracts or agreements providing for the furnishing of personal property or the performance of labor for the organization.
>
> 5.   Keeps full and accurate accounts of disbursements of organization funds.
>
> 6.   Pays to organization officers or employees such salaries as they are entitled to.

Sometimes the bylaws will provide that the clerk is to make a periodic report as to business on the chairman's table. (1 HP Sec. 252.) Or they may require him to keep records pertaining to the financial affairs of the organization, especially where it has no treasurer. He may, for example, be required to prepare an itemized statement of expenditures from available funds, the expenditures of the organization at the end of each fiscal year, and/or a complete statement of his receipts and expenditures as clerk. (1 HP Sec. 253.)

Sec. 50. Sergeant at Arms; Doorkeeper

Many membership organizations are of such nature that one of its officers should be designated as the sergeant at arms. If so, his duties should be set forth in the bylaws. (See Rule IV, House

Rules.) His main responsibility is to maintain order during meetings under the direction of the presiding officer. As the sergeant at arms, he is also charged with the duty of enforcing regulations designed to preserve the peace and security of the organization and to protect its real and personal property. (1 HP Sec. 258.)

In relatively large organizations with restricted memberships, or those that sit frequently in executive session, a doorkeeper is a necessity. In such organizations the duties of this officer should be set out in the bylaws and may include the following: checking credentials of persons seeking entrance to organization meetings; enforcing rules governing attendance at the meeting place of the organization; and maintaining custody of furniture, books, and other property belonging to the organization.

Sec. 51. Board of Directors

A capable and loyal board of directors is essential to the successful growth and development of any membership organization. The vigor and skill of the board in assuming its responsibilities will determine in large measure the character of the entire organization. If the board is active and capable, this tends to bring about a proper balance between the members, the board, and the chief executive or manager. But if the board is indifferent, there is a likelihood that the manager or chief executive will take over most of its functions, resulting in a "one-man" organization with a "rubber-stamp" board.

A strong, responsible, well-balanced board of directors can do much to ensure the success of any membership organization. By the same token, a board that is weak, indecisive, or unevenly balanced can ruin an organization or greatly impair its effectiveness. Power struggles within the board can be extremely unhealthy. This can be counteracted by having board membership changed from time to time, but in such a way as not to sacrifice the continuity that should exist from one board to another. This and other measures intended to keep the board in good health and on an even keel are shown in the provisions below, which should be reflected in the bylaws.

  1. Staggered terms of office so that not all experienced directors go off the board in the same year.
  2. A nominating committee to present a panel of nominees at the annual meeting when the directors are elected.

3.   No director should serve on this committee; it should be drawn entirely from the membership.
4.   Requiring at least two nominees for each vacancy on the board.
5.   Allowing nominations from the floor at the annual meeting or, in the alternative, allowing written nominations from members submitted prior to the annual meeting.
6.   Voting by the membership by secret ballot; this avoids subsequent retaliation by a disgruntled director against a member who might have voted against him.

The size of the board of directors varies greatly from organization to organization. In smaller ones the board usually has a membership of five, seven, or nine. From this group it is customary to select the officers of the organization. In larger associations, and especially in regional or other large-scale organizations, the boards usually consist of larger numbers up to as many as fifty or sixty persons.

The criteria for determining the makeup of the board of directors are of great importance. In some organizations the geographical area served by the organization is broken up into districts, with a director elected from each district. In other organizations the directors are elected on the basis of the particular products with which the organization is concerned, as in the case of farmer cooperatives.

A board makeup that is limited to a geographical or district representation has its limitations, the primary one being that such directors are too far removed from the local membership. In such a case, where the directors are chosen on a district basis by delegates from locals, it may be desirable to set up a system of advisory boards. These boards keep in touch with the local membership and help develop member-relations programs. Such boards do not make policy. They meet with the local managers, work with committees, and serve as liaison between the central board of directors and local members.

It is important to recognize that a board of directors is a body that functions in much the same way as a committee. Activities of any board member become official only when he acts through the entire board. However, the work of the board may be divided among a number of special or permanent committees, each dealing with some phase of the organization's operations. For example, there may be a finance committee, a membership committee, and others. Each committee studies the problems in each particular field and makes recommendations to the full board. In some instances, committees may be given certain powers to act for the board, subject to its review.

In many organizations a relatively small group from the board, usually consisting of three or five members, is selected to serve as an executive committee. This committee performs various duties authorized by the board, provided such authorization is permitted under the bylaws.

It is of utmost importance that each member of the board of directors conduct himself in such a way as to avoid any possible conflict of interest. Each must always put the interests of the organization first. This means that, ordinarily, directors may not be employed by the organization or receive compensation from it except in the performance of specific duties directly connected with their positions as directors.

Retirement

The founders of a membership organization should face at the outset the question as to whether the directors should be subject to mandatory retirement. At issue in such a plan is whether the bringing in of new blood and new ideas to the board is sufficiently advantageous to offset the disadvantage of losing the skills of the most experienced members of the board through mandatory retirement.

For whatever reason, most membership organizations do not specify a retirement age for the directors in their bylaws. Only a few organizations have mandatory retirement plans for directors, but those that do enforce them rigidly.

In any event, a mandatory retirement plan, if adopted at all, should be adopted at the inception of the birth of the organization. It is invariably difficult to propose a mandatory retirement plan without offending someone on the board who might be affected by such a provision.

At least a partial solution to this dilemma is to adopt a bylaw requiring the retirement from service of directors at the age of seventy, but retaining them as veteran directors so that their advice and counsel will remain available to the board. Such a bylaw is set out below:

> All Directors of the Board shall retire from active service to the
> Board upon attainment of the age of seventy (70), and each Direc-

tor shall automatically at that time become a Veteran Director for life. All Veteran Directors shall have the same rights as other Directors on the Board, excepting the right to vote, and shall have all the privileges and benefits of the office, including fees for attendance at meetings of the Board.

Sec. 52. Kinds of Directors

Most membership organizations have a board of directors that is elected, not appointed. But the bylaws of some of them provide for the appointment of certain directors, and a few have directors on the board in both categories. In still other organizations the directors, other than those elected by the membership, serve only as observers or advisers to the board, and fall into the nonvoting category.

In addition to the classifications of elective and appointive, voting and nonvoting, there are various subcategories useful in describing those chosen to establish the policies of a membership organization. They are: (1) public directors, (2) honorary directors, (3) alternate directors, (4) directors at large, and (5) veteran directors.

Public Directors

As the term is used among membership organizations, a public director is one who serves on the board of an organization that is looked upon as being vested with a public interest. As the term implies, public directors are charged with the responsibility of guarding the interests of the general public. They are more common in organizations that have interests outside of their immediate membership.

In some states it is a statutory requirement that public directors sit on the boards of membership organizations in which the public has an interest. Farmer cooperatives, for example, are typically covered by such legislation. In other states the bylaws of a membership organization may provide for public directors even though there is no state statute on the subject.

Public directors are either appointed or elected. If elected, public directors are put in office by the membership. They may, but need not, be members of the organization, and generally have the same voting power and serve for the same term of office as the elected directors.

A bylaw typical of those providing for the appointment of public directors is set out below.

> There shall be two Public Directors for each state in which the Association operates. These Public Directors shall be appointed, each for a term of two years, on a staggered basis, by the Dean of the State University of the state from which such Public Directors are to be appointed. Public Directors need not be members of the Association.

Another form for such a bylaw is as follows:

> In addition to the elected Directors provided for herein, there shall be one Public Director to be selected jointly by the chief officer of the State Bar Association and the President of the Law School of the State University.

Honorary Directors

A number of membership organizations provide in their bylaws for honorary directors. Honorary directors generally serve strictly in an advisory capacity. They are often appointed as a taken of recognition, and have no vote. A bylaw typical of those providing for honorary directors is set out below.

> The Board of Directors of this Association shall have the power to appoint no more than three Honorary Directors, who shall serve without a vote. None of the provisions of these bylaws shall be construed to apply to such Honorary Directors. Their presence or absence at a meeting is not to affect the ascertainment of a quorum.

Alternate Directors

An alternate director is a person who is capable under the bylaws of filling a vacancy among the regular directors, or who can take the place of a regular director when the latter is unable to attend a meeting of the board. In the case of a federated membership organization, or one with geographical representation on its board, a vacancy occurring on the board is filled by appointment of the alternate director from the district where the vacancy occurred. The alternate serves until the next annual meeting when a permanent director is elected to fill out the balance of the unexpired term. A typical bylaw providing for alternate directors is set out below.

> One Alternate Director shall be elected at the annual meeting for each District from which a Director has been elected, the nomi-

nation and election of such alternate to be conducted in the same manner as the nomination and election of Directors. The terms of office of such alternates shall be one year or until their successors have been elected and qualified.

Directors at Large

In a few of the larger membership organizations, especially those that are federated or regional in nature, provision is made in the bylaws for directors at large. The primary distinction between directors at large and regular directors is that the former are elected to represent the entire territory served by the organization rather than any particular district or area. Their function is to spread representation, to deemphasize the interests of limited geographical areas, and to look to the broader objectives of the organization as such. Directors at large are elected by the entire membership. They have the same standing and voting power as any other elected director, in the absence of any limitations in the bylaws to this effect. The bylaw below is illustrative of those providing for the election of directors at large.

> This Association shall be managed by a Board of nine Directors. One Director shall be elected from each of the Association's eight districts. The ninth Director shall be elected at large by vote of the membership at the annual meeting.

Veteran Directors

At least a partial solution to the dilemma posed by mandatory retirement plans is to adopt a bylaw requiring the retirement from service of directors at the age of seventy, but retaining them as "Veteran Directors" so that their advice and counsel will remain available to the board. Such a bylaw is set out above. (See Sec. 51.)

Sec. 53. Duties and Responsibilities

The board of directors of a membership organization has as its primary duty the management of the organization and the direction of its operations in accordance with policies previously agreed upon and duly adopted. The board represents the members in the overall conduct of the affairs of the organization. In this capacity it sets policies and programs, employs a manager or a chief executive, and reviews the operations of the organization from time to time to make sure that they are in keeping with the organization's goals and objectives.

The powers and duties of directors of membership organiža-
tions should always be spelled out in the bylaws, as shown below.
But they are responsible to the membership for the proper conduct
of the affairs of the organization whether this duty is imposed on
them by the bylaws or not. The responsibility for the success or
failure of the organization is always vested in its elected directors.

The board of directors of a membership organization is invariably vested with the power of general supervision and control of its
business and its affairs. The bylaws may provide, for example:

> The Board of Directors shall have general supervision and control
> of the business and affairs of the Association and shall establish all
> policies and make all rules and regulations for the management of
> its business and guidance of members, officers, employees, and
> agents.

In exercising this overall power of control, the board ordinarily has the following general duties and responsibilities:

Trustee function. The directors act as trustees for the members they represent. Essentially they are custodians and are
charged with safeguarding and managing the assets entrusted to
them. As trustees, they must act in the interests of all members
and not on their own behalf.

Establishing general policies. The directors are charged with
the responsibility of developing long-run objectives and long-range
plans. The directors must anticipate the future needs of the membership and ascertain the economic feasibility of satisfying those
needs.

Employ a chief executive or manager. The success or failure of
a membership organization will often hinge on the decision made
by the board in hiring a chief executive to manage the organization.
The board must set forth clear-cut policies for him to follow and
delegate sufficient authority to him.

Financial responsibilities. It is the duty of the board of directors to insist that an adequate bookkeeping system be established
and maintained. The board should also require external audits of
the accounts of the organization. It must then arrange for a presentation of the results of the audit to the members, which is usually
done at the annual meeting. In other words, the board reports
directly to the membership on the financial status of the organization. It is important that the audit be initiated by the board, in its
trusteeship role, rather than the manager.

Allocating organization income. The bylaws should indicate clearly how net savings and other income are to be distributed or allocated, and the board should follow these bylaws to the letter. In some organizations, such as farmer cooperatives and other similar institutions, some portion of net savings will accrue directly to the members. Distribution of this income by the board may be in the form of stock dividends. And the board should make some allocation of savings to organization reserves, if so authorized.

In addition to these general powers of supervision and control, a board of directors has many specific duties and responsibilities. Some are implied from the general authority vested in the board, and some are imposed on them by specific direction of the bylaws. Ordinarily, the board, collectively and individually, must:

1.   Decide how the resources and services of the organization are to be used for the benefit of members.

2.   Attend board meetings; and each director, though not present, shares responsibility for board decisions.

3.   Represent all members and inform themselves as to the needs of the membership as a whole.

4.   Understand the articles of incorporation or charter of the organization and its bylaws, making sure that business is conducted within authorized limitations.

5.   Appoint, generally supervise, and remove at will agents and other employees of the organization selected by the board; the board also prescribes their duties and salaries and may require them to give bond. (See Sec. 28 *supra*.)

6.   Employ a competent manager and set out guidelines within which he is to exercise his duties.

7.   Establish sound operational policies and objectives and review the progress of the organization regularly.

8.   Supervise the preparation of the operating budget at the beginning of each fiscal year.

9.   Supervise the production of financial statements at the end of each fiscal year and require monthly financial reports and operating statements.

10.   Select banks or similar institutions for the deposit of the funds of the organization and designate persons who are to sign checks for the organization.

11.   Borrow funds for various purposes authorized by the articles of incorporation or charter.

12.   Supervise the maintenance of an adequate bookkeeping and accounting system.

13.   Present to the membership at stated periods the statement of the financial condition and operations of the organization.

14.   Approve all important contractual or financial undertakings of the organization (members of the board of directors can be held financially responsible for negligence or breach of trust in such matters).

15.   Enter into or authorize contracts with suppliers of goods and services required by members.

16.   Employ a qualified auditor to audit the books at least once a year and report on his findings.

17.   Supervise the preparation of plans for the annual meeting of the organization.

18.   Call special meetings of the membership when the board deems it advisable, or upon a proper request of the members in accordance with the bylaws.

19.   Review annually the insurance policies that are carried by the organization and evaluate the status of fidelity bonds on the chief executive and other key employees.

There is some question as to whether a director should limit his participation to the policy level or should take an active personal role in keeping members informed of the organization's affairs. There are some advantages to be gained by giving directors the responsibility for developing a member-relations program and in communicating generally with the members. For example, the attendance at committee and general membership meetings is a part of a director's member-relations job. These meetings give directors a chance to talk with the members and to share and present opinions. A director should also frequently represent his organization at regional and state meetings, leadership conferences, and the like.

Service on special committees is also a desirable responsibility for a director. If he serves as chairman of a committee, it gives him a chance to participate actively in member-relations work, both in the committee sessions themselves and in presenting oral and written reports from the committee to the general membership.

On the other hand, director participation in a member-relations program is potentially dangerous and should not be undertaken without an evaluation of the risks involved. For example, asking a member for advice or suggestions may also turn out to be a direct route to trouble. If a director seeks out the advice of the membership, he will, as a policy-maker, be expected to act on the advice. And since the advice he receives will quite likely be as diverse as the number of his advisers, there will be no way in which he can satisfy everybody.

The surveys of members' opinions are more appropriately conducted by the executive director or managerial staff rather than one or more members of the board of directors. The management staff can distill the views of members into a recommendation to the board of directors, but it cannot be charged with errors of policy because it is not responsible for making policy.

Sec. 54. Managers and Other Employees

Every membership organization must have someone whose function it is to carry out the policies of the board of directors or membership. This person is usually called a chief executive, executive director, or manager. The term "hired management" is normally used to include the manager together with other key personnel who are delegated management functions.

For any given organization, various managerial and staff structures are possible. Each will have its advantages and disadvantages. It is the task of the chief executive, together with the board of directors, to analyze the different possible structures and to select the one that seems the most promising.

For example, where the need for a given line of services has increased and the management has decided to establish a new department to handle them, the chief executive (together with the board) should hire someone to take charge of the newly created department; new lines of authority and new job descriptions will be needed to reflect these changes.

Personnel administration is an essential responsibility of management in the membership organization. Dealing constructively with personnel problems reflects good management and contributes to the success of the entire organization. Good personnel administration involves the entire management team—the board of directors, the executive director or general manager, and any supervisory staff.

Personnel recruitment is a problem with which the chief executive must deal. Most employees who work below the policy-making level in industry generally can be switched from one type of business to another with no appreciable difference in the technical performance of the job. However, membership organizations have found that familiarity with their objectives and goals is a desirable job requirement, in addition to technical skills, particularly for employees who come in contact with members.

Although the establishment of effective policies for recruiting, training, and evaluating employees is no easy task for small membership organizations, or for new and inexperienced ones, guidance in this area is available. One source of information and assistance can be found among larger, similar organizations with well-developed personnel procedures. And although no literature exists on the personnel problems of membership organizations as such, a considerable body of information is available on personnel administration for business enterprises generally. This may be obtained from such sources as universities, trade associations, state employment services, and the federal Small Business Administration.

The chief executive or manager must also be well informed as to the articles of incorporation, as well as the bylaws. He should also have an understanding of the provisions of the applicable statute. Often legal authority is drawn from general corporation laws of the state, and some basic understanding of these statutory provisions is important.

Other areas in which the manager must become knowledgeable include such labor-related matters as union practices, collective bargaining, current labor legislation, and court decisions. Information on these subjects is available from the National Labor Relations Board, 1717 Pennsylvania Avenue, N.W., Washington, D.C. 20570, and from its forty-two regional and local offices.

The need for acquiring such expertise on the part of the manager becomes especially acute when the organization has no staff attorney. Unfortunately, most membership organizations do not have an attorney on the staff who acts as legal counsel. Most of them retain independent legal counsel, however, and many of them retain an attorney on an "as-needed" basis. Where an attorney is a staff employee, he may be given such additional responsibilities as approving minutes of the board, being present at certain committee meetings, and the like.

Conflicts of Interest

Ethical and other considerations dictate that the chief executive and his employees avoid any possible conflict of interest. Organizational employees should have no interest in any corporation or firm with which the organization does business. They should avoid any arrangement by which they could exploit their organization's connections to their personal advantage.

As a matter of general policy, and to avoid a possible conflict of interest, no board member should serve or act as the chief executive or manager of the organization, except perhaps for a temporary period of very short duration. If a member of the board is elected manager, he should resign his position from the board. This is because he would be called upon to act as a board member to approve or disapprove his own acts as manager, thereby creating an unfortunate conflict of interest.

Sec. 55. Duties and Responsibilities

The responsibility in a membership organization for executing the many details of its operation rests with the chief executive and his key employees. Naturally, the specific duties and responsibilities of the chief executive or manager will vary with the type of organization, the character of services rendered by it, its size, and any special conditions under which it operates.

In larger organizations the chief executive's duties are managerial and coordinative in character, as various departments are usually headed by a department supervisor. In smaller organizations the chief executive or manager and a few aides will shoulder even the most menial of operational chores. But in every membership organization, large or small, sound procedure requires that the chief executive or manager have certain definite responsibilities. Set out below is a list of the most important ones.

1.   Supervising the operations of the organization in a manner consistent with the powers delegated by the board and working in close cooperation with the directors.

2.   Complying with the organization's policies and conducting the affairs of the organization along guidelines established and approved by the board.

3.   Establishing short-range plans and programs pursuant to the general long-range policies that have been laid down by the board.

4.   Assisting the board of directors in setting up new policies, in evaluating the value and utility of policies previously adopted, and in determining the need for change or modification in existing policies.

5.   Obtaining assistants and other employees qualified to exe-

cute the work of the organization and supervising and coordinating their activities.

6.   Developing a budget of anticipated receipts and expected operating costs and making necessary adjustments in monthly expenditures so that they will always be held to amounts budgeted.

7.   Maintaining adequate accounting records of all transactions needed in any evaluation of the financial position of the organization at any time.

8.   Preparing data and reports so that the organization's operations can be compared with similar data for previous operating periods.

9.   Developing membership loyalty and confidence in the organization and keeping members informed as to progress.

Sec. 56. Duties of Board and Manager Distinguished

The allocation of duties and responsibilities between the board of directors and the chief executive or manager is often a difficult and complex question. Much depends upon local circumstances, size and nature of the organization, and the abilities and personalities of those involved.

Normally, the board sets the organization's policies and objectives, and the manager is responsible for planning a program that will carry out those policies and objectives. Experience has shown that the board of directors should not interfere with the day-to-day management of the organization and that the manager should not attempt to set policies. Each has a separate function to perform.

The board of directors, on its part, must assume full responsibility for developing the policies of the organization and evaluating the results obtained from their implementation. But this does not mean that the chief executive and his assistants do not have important roles in the development and administration of policies. The board must in fact rely to a great extent on information, factual data, and the advice and suggestions furnished by the chief executive and his staff. The board may also delegate certain duties to the chief executive or someone on his staff, though the final responsibility therefor remains with the board.

In delegating duties to the chief executive, the board must circumscribe his areas of responsibility and give to him various powers within those areas. The board must then periodically review his activities to make sure that the organization's policies are being implemented. In so doing, the board should not turn from its major responsibility as a policy-making body to concern itself with the routine details of the organization's affairs. The development of a busybody attitude on the part of the board reduces its effectiveness and may create an intolerable situation for the chief executive or manager.

Some general tests to determine areas of responsibility are set out below, not as absolutes, but as guides.

Time-period test. Some decisions in an organization are by nature intended to apply for a relatively short period of time, whereas others have implications extending over a relatively long period of time. Thus, the length of time is important in determining the allocation of responsibilities between the manager and the board of directors. Long-run decisions are invariably made by the board. For example, the setting of goals of the organization, the making of long-range plans, the establishing of basic policies, are usually characterized by their long-run nature and must be made by the board. Increases in the staff or enlargement of facilities are also the board's responsibility. On the other hand, the chief executive would have the responsibility for making decisions in many of these same areas, but covering much shorter periods of time.

Concept/action test. For the purpose of allocating responsibility, a decision may be classified as one involving a concept or as one involving an action. In dealing with concepts, one makes proposals, establishes plans, estimates probable outcome. Such activities involve concepts, not actions, and fall within the responsibility of the board of directors.

Trusteeship test. Since the directors are trustees, elected to act on behalf of the membership as a whole, any decision involving the safety of the property of the membership is a trusteeship decision and falls within the responsibility of the board. The board cannot delegate to the manager such things as effective financial controls, arranging for external audits, or determining the distribution of organization income. The board may delegate some of its duties in this respect, but it cannot shift its basic responsibility. For example, the board may give the manager authority to purchase insurance coverage on organization property, but it cannot delegate its authority for safeguarding the property of the organization.

Control test. Control activities within an organization may be divided. Control procedures in a membership organization may be divided into two kinds, primary and secondary. Primary controls are those dealing with long-range activities or those involving the trusteeship responsibilities of the board. They include controls over the chief executive, long-range financial commitments, and controls for overall performance of the organization. Secondary controls, on the other hand, are concerned with short-run operational aspects of the organization. These include control over subordinate employees, including department heads, and office procedures. In general, the board of directors must assume responsibility for primary controls, and the hired management assumes responsibility for secondary controls.

Management-function test. One general guideline that is useful in allocating hiring responsibilities is as follows: The manager is employed by the board, whereas employees having no management responsibilities are hired by the manager. However, many positions within the organization are often of dual nature, in which case staffing should be assumed as a joint responsibility of the manager and the board. Department heads, for example, will often share certain managerial duties with the chief executive. In such cases, therefore, it is advisable for the manager to staff these positions with the approval of the board.

Sec. 57. Removal of Officers and Employees

In the U.S. House of Representatives the Speaker may be removed "at the will" of the House. (See House Rules Sec. 315.) This is consistent with the general rule prevailing in most states that an officer may be removed by the persons who elected or appointed him whenever, in their judgment, the best interests of the organization will be served thereby. The courts will not interfere with such a decision in the absence of a strong showing that the action taken was manifestly unfair or against the public interest.[3] This rule should be embodied in the bylaws, as follows:

> Any elected or appointed officer may be removed at will by those persons who elected or appointed him by majority vote, whenever it is in the best interests of the organization, or for cause.

Charges against an officer that may be made the subject of an investigation and possible removal include the betrayal of executive secrets, the corrupt use of power in appointing subordinates, neglect of duty, misappropriation of funds, official misconduct, improper administration of funds, or alteration or falsification of records. (1 HP Secs. 284-96.) Authorship of published statements

[3] See 6 Am Jur 2d *Associations and Clubs* Sec. 9.

prejudicial to the reputations of members is also considered good cause for removal. (6 CP Sec. 37.) And where there is evidence of financial irregularity in the conduct of the affairs of an organization, the membership may by resolution appoint a select committee to investigate the matter. For example, if an unexplained deficit appears in the cash reserves of an officer, a committee may be appointed to examine the accounts of the office. (1 HP Sec. 293.)

Ordinarily, the conduct that is the basis for an officer's removal is conduct *while in office*, and not something that may have occurred prior to his election or appointment. On the other hand, the membership may take appropriate action against an officer notwithstanding the prior submission of a resignation by the officer involved. In other words, he cannot stop the removal procedure simply by offering his resignation. (1 HP Sec. 292.)

The procedure leading to the removal of an officer should be initiated by those persons who elected or appointed him in the first place. If he was appointed by the board of directors, that body should initiate the action; if the officer was elected by the membership, the action should be initiated by motion of a member in good standing during a regular business meeting of the organization. It should also be pointed out that an officer against whom certain charges have been made may himself petition the membership to initiate an inquiry as to their validity. (1 HP Secs. 294, 295.)

There have been instances in which an accused officer has appeared before the full membership to respond to oral interrogation by it, in which case the rule is that any member may rise to propound a question. (6 HP Sec. 37.) This procedure is not recommended, however, being neither fair to the accused officer, who should be given the opportunity of a closed hearing, nor to the membership at large, which is not equipped to conduct the detailed investigation such cases deserve. The better practice is to refer the matter to a special committee for a thorough, careful investigation. And although an officer may be suspended from the exercise of his functions pending an investigation or examination of the charges made (1 HP Sec. 287), the membership should await the report of the investigating committee before considering a resolution calling for the removal of the officer in question. (1 HP Secs. 290, 292.)

After the committee has completed its investigation of the matter, it should offer its findings to the membership along with its recommendation as to action to be taken, if any. (1 HP Sec. 290.)

In the event that the findings of the committee exonerate the officer in question, then such findings should be printed or otherwise circulated among the membership. (1 HP Sec. 295.)

If, after a full and fair investigation, the committee reports adversely on the conduct of a particular officer, the membership may then take action in several ways. It may discharge or dismiss the officer, suspend him with or without pay, initiate civil or criminal proceedings against him, or declare his office vacant. (1 HP Secs. 284-96.) The fact that the bylaws provide for the existence of such offices does not mean that they cannot be declared vacant or that successors must be appointed. (6 CP Sec. 36.)

Before taking formal punitive action, a membership organization should afford the accused officer the opportunity of offering such explanation or evidence as he might desire. He should also be afforded the opportunity to consult counsel (6 CP Sec. 37) and to prepare and present evidence in his defense (1 HP Secs. 284-96).

Finally, when an officer is charged with misconduct and a resolution calling for his removal is presented to the membership, the individual involved may by unanimous consent be permitted to address the membership in his own defense. (1 HP Secs. 287, 296.)

With respect to the removal of a subordinate of an officer, it is settled that when authority is granted to a designated officer to appoint any person in his discretion to an office, and the bylaws do not give the incumbent a right to hold the office for any specified period, the power of removal and of filling the vacancy thereby made is incidental to the authority to appoint. (6 CP Sec. 36.) Therefore, when an officer of the organization exercises his authority to remove one of his subordinates, he need not bring the matter before the membership, and the membership should not interfere with his action (1 HP Sec. 249), at least in the absence of a showing that the officer abused his discretion.

Sec. 58. Resolutions and Motions

A membership organization may seek the removal of one or more of its officers by a resolution that is presented to and voted on by the membership. This resolution may be in simple form, as follows:

> *Resolved*, That Robert E. Smith, the Doorkeeper of [NAME OF ORGANIZATION], be, and he is hereby, discharged.

Or the resolution may indicate the cause for removal, as follows:

> *Resolved*, That John W. Jones, the Clerk of [NAME OF ORGANIZATION], by directing the alteration of certain documents

and the falsification of certain records of this organization in violation of parliamentary law and of his sworn duty, should be, and is hereby, removed from the office of Clerk. [See 1 HP Secs. 284, 285.]

Resolutions calling for the removal of an officer should ordinarily be referred to a special investigating committee, with the officer in question being suspended from office pending the outcome of the investigation. In such cases the resolution of referral to committee may take the following form:

Resolved, That the pending resolution be referred to the Committee on Rules, with power to consider the complaint against [NAME OF ACCUSED OFFICER], and to reinstate, reprimand, or dismiss said official. [6 CP Sec. 37.]

In those cases where referral to a committee is inappropriate, a member may offer a motion from the floor that the officer in question vacate his office and that the membership proceed to the election of his successor. In the event that the office in question is that of the presiding officer, he cannot arbitrarily refuse to permit a motion by any member that he vacate that office and that the membership choose a new presiding officer. (6 CP Sec. 35.)

An organization may remove an officer by a resolution declaring the office in question vacant and transferring the duties of the officer involved to another official in the organization. Such a resolution may declare, for example:

Resolved, That the office of Doorkeeper be vacated by its present incumbent and that the duties of the Doorkeeper be, and the same are hereby, evolved upon the Sergeant at Arms until otherwise ordered. [1 HP Sec. 288.]

Or the accused officer's assistant may be directed to perform the duties of the office (1 HP Sec. 292), in which case the resolution could read as follows:

Resolved, That the office of Clerk be, and the same is hereby, declared vacant; and that the Assistant Clerk be, and he is hereby, directed to perform the duties of the Clerk until a successor shall be elected and duly qualified.

Under such a resolution, the salary of the officer in question terminates as of the date the office is declared vacant. (6 CP Sec. 36.)

The removal or ouster of an officer may also be accomplished indirectly simply by the abolition of his office. This may be brought about by a resolution, as follows:

Resolved, That [TITLE OF OFFICE] is not necessary for the service of this organization and that the same is hereby abolished.

A resolution calling for the removal of an officer of an organization raises a question of privilege (1 HP Sec. 284), as does a resolution proposing that the office of an officer be declared vacant (6 CP Sec. 35). It should be borne in mind in this regard, however, that while a resolution calling for the removal of an officer is privileged, a resolution calling for the appointment of a certain person to fill an office is not.

ELECTIONS

Sec. 59. Election of Officers

The election of a presiding officer is initiated by motion (1 Hinds' Precedents[1] Sec. 210) or resolution (1 HP Sec. 214). Nominations for the office may be made from the floor, simply by naming the candidates, or by one or more of a wide variety of more formal and complex nominating procedures. (See Secs. 62-70 *infra*.) These candidates may be asked to state their views before proceeding to the election, and a resolution to that effect may be offered by any member. Such a resolution may take the following form:

> *Resolved*, That it is the duty of all candidates for the office of Chairman to state their opinions frankly and fully upon questions involved in their election, especially when interrogated by the membership.

Answers by candidates to interrogatories from the membership are regarded as sufficient compliance with such a resolution. (1 HP Sec. 218.)

The election of the remaining officers of the organization, such as the treasurer, clerk, sergeant at arms, and doorkeeper, is next in order, and is generally brought about by resolution. (1 HP Sec. 81.)

Where officers are to be elected by resolution, the resolution may contain as many paragraphs as there are officers to be elected, each in this form:

> *Resolved*, That [NAME OF CANDIDATE] be, and hereby is, chosen [TITLE OF OFFICE] of [NAME OF ORGANIZATION] to hold office until another is chosen in his stead. [1 HP Secs. 81, 193.]

Additional paragraphs may be added to reflect the candidacy of other individuals for other offices that are being voted upon. (1 HP Sec. 81.) Of course, if some members wish to propose a different slate of nominees, they may do so by offering a similar resolution, which may be moved as a substitute. (1 HP Secs. 81, 196, 197.)

[1]Hereinafter cited as HP.

The bylaws should indicate whether officers are to be elected by written resolution or *viva voce*—that is, pursuant to a motion made orally from the floor. An election by resolution is not in compliance with a rule requiring election of officers by a *viva voce* procedure. (1 HP Sec. 191.) In any event, in the absence of bylaw requirements, it is the membership, and not the holdover clerk, who decides by what method the organization shall proceed to elect a chairman. (1 HP Sec. 210.)

A motion or resolution that the organization proceed to the election of an officer is debatable, until the previous question is ordered. (1 HP Sec. 213.) While that motion or resolution is pending, another question of privilege may not be presented. (1 HP Sec. 214.) This means that the motion to proceed to the election of a chairman, being privileged, takes precedence over a question concerning the right of a particular member to be seated. (1 HP Sec. 212.) Thus, although the right of a member to participate in the election also raises a question of privilege, it is secondary to the question of higher privilege raised by a motion to proceed to the election of a chairman. (1 HP Sec. 214.)

A resolution to proceed to the election of an officer must be made at the time specified in the bylaws for holding such elections. And if the membership postpones an election of an officer until a day certain, a resolution to proceed to the election is not in order before that day. (1 HP Sec. 263.)

The presiding officer should announce the results of the voting as soon as the count is complete. This announcement may be followed by a short installation service and a few brief remarks from one or more of the new officers and directors. The presiding officer should express the appreciation of the organization to the retiring directors and losing nominees. No debate or business is in order during that period of time after the election of a chairman and before he has assumed the chair. (1 HP Sec. 219.)

Sec. 60. Election of Directors

One of the first duties of the members after a new membership organization comes into existence is to elect a board of directors. From then on, the members elect directors at the regular annual meeting.

The bylaws of a membership organization may require that nominees for election to the board of directors possess certain qualifications, such as residence in a particular state or district.

State laws may also impose various requirements in this regard. Under the laws of some states, for example, the board of directors of a membership organization must be drawn from the membership itself. Even where not required by state statute, organizations will frequently make membership a qualification of becoming a director.

The modern trend, however, appears to favor liberalization of those bylaws making membership a qualification of sitting on the board. As an organization grows in size, becomes more integrated, and develops more complex operations, greater consideration is given to the desirability of not having a board of directors composed exclusively of members. In fact, there appears to be a distinct willingness to explore the possibility of broadening the representation on the board to include people from many other walks of life.

In view of the many important responsibilities of the board of directors, members should weigh carefully the merits and qualifications of any nominee before they elect him to serve on the board. Ordinarily, any member of the organization meeting the requirements stated in the bylaws may be eligible for election to the board; this does not mean, however, that every member is actually fitted to serve as a director. The bylaws usually contain only one eligibility requirement for board membership, and that is that the person be a member in good standing. But there are other prerequisites of even greater importance—namely, ability, judgment, and experience. Moreover, in the interests of obtaining a well-rounded and balanced board of directors, the members should consider as nominees individuals who have had specialized training or experience in such fields as law, finance, and economics.

Sec. 61. Special Elections

If the office of the presiding officer becomes vacant, as by the death or resignation of the chairman, the organization may adjourn or proceed to a special election of a new chairman. The election of a new chairman is initiated by resolution. Such a resolution is of high privilege. (1 HP Sec. 234.) The form for such a resolution is as follows:

> Whereas the membership being informed that since its last adjournment [NAME OF CHAIRMAN], who had been elected Chairman, has departed this life, creating a vacancy in the office of Chairman; therefore

> *Resolved*, That this membership do now proceed to the election of a Chairman *viva voce*. [1 HP Sec. 234.]

Likewise, when an officer other than the chairman dies, the vacancy is ordinarily filled by an election pursuant to a resolution adopted by the membership. Such a resolution may take the following form:

> *Resolved*, That F. B. Jones be, and is hereby, chosen [TITLE OF OFFICE] to fill the vacancy caused by the death of the late W. J. Smith. [1 HP Sec. 267.]

A resolution providing for the election of an officer following a resignation of the incumbent may take the following form:

> *Resolved*, That this organization now proceed to the election of a [TITLE OF OFFICE] in place of [NAME OF RESIGNED OFFICER], resigned. [See 1 HP Sec. 264.]

> or

> *Resolved*, That this organization will, on Thursday next, at 12:30 o'clock, proceed to the election of a [TITLE OF OFFICE] to fill the vacancy occasioned by the resignation of [NAME OF RESIGNED OFFICER]. [1 HP Sec. 265.]

The bylaws may also make provision for the possibility of all of its officers resigning or being killed in an accident. Such a bylaw is set out below:

> In the event that the entire Board of Directors shall resign or die, any twenty-five (25) members may call a special meeting in the same manner that the Chief Officer may call such a meeting, and Directors for the unexpired term may be elected at such special meeting in the manner provided for their election at annual meetings.

A member elected to fill a vacancy serves no longer time than the remainder of the term of the officer whose place he takes. (1 HP Sec. 3.)

Sec. 62. Nominating Procedures

Membership organizations nominate candidates for elective offices in many different ways. The bylaws usually spell out these procedures, though there are a few organizations that have deliberately omitted any mention whatever of nominating procedures in their bylaws.

In fact, in some organizations voting is by ballot without the formality of nominations either from a committee or from the membership. The members simply write in the name of their choice for each vacant position. This procedure is not recommended, even for relatively small organizations, because it generates the names of too many different candidates, some of whom may be unwilling to accept the office, and it often leads to time-consuming runoff elections.

Where the bylaws are silent in this respect, the membership has the opportunity to choose any legal method of nominating and electing officers. This makes it possible to change nomination procedures at any annual meeting. During one given year, for example, the membership of such an organization may nominate their directors by voice from the floor at the annual meeting. The next year, following criticism that the voice procedure results in spur-of-the-moment nominations that do not produce the best-qualified individuals, the membership may, without amending the bylaws, vote to use a nominating committee in choosing its directors, with members having the privilege of supplementing the nominations of the committee by nominations from the floor. This method may work so well that the membership may vote to continue it the following year.

By deliberately omitting from the bylaws specific nominating procedures, the membership introduces flexibility in the method of choosing candidates. This has both advantages and disadvantages. Its desirability is that the membership may change its nomination procedures at any time without having to amend the bylaws. The organization may adopt the newest and most advanced nominating procedures immediately during any given annual meeting. The disadvantage of the plan is that where the bylaws do not spell out some continuity in nominating procedures, the stability of the organization is impaired to that extent.

It is usually desirable that two or more candidates be nominated for each vacancy to be filled. But sometimes organizational structure and bylaw provisions preclude the nomination of more than one candidate for each vacancy. For example, where the bylaws provide for a ten-man board of directors, and requires each candidate to be a manager of one of its ten districts, there is no chance to nominate two candidates for each vacancy.

The absence of provisions requiring the nomination of at least two candidates for each vacancy will ordinarily contribute to membership apathy and disinterest. With only one candidate for each position, the membership has no choice. Such elections turn out to be cut-and-dried affairs, with the membership recognizing them as such.

Nomination of Directors at Large

In many federated or regional organizations, directors at large are nominated by a public institution or agency, such as a state university. In other instances directors at large are nominated from the floor at annual membership meetings. In still other instances such nominations are made by the incumbent directors. The bylaw below is illustrative of the type that permits directors at large to be nominated by incumbent directors.

> The Board of Directors shall, by majority vote of its members at its annual meeting, elect three Directors at Large. Any person, whether or not a member of the Association, shall be eligible for election to such office and shall have the same rights, powers, liabilities, and duties as all other Directors. They shall hold office for a term of two years and until their successors are elected and qualified.

Sec. 63. Nominations from the Floor

The nomination of candidates for election by voice from the floor is one of the oldest methods for selecting nominees, with origins in British parliamentary practice. Today, the bylaws of many membership organizations provide for nominations from the floor, either exclusively or in combination with other methods. In fact, most membership organizations include in their bylaws a general supplementary stipulation providing for nominations from the floor in addition to other specified nominating procedures, or as an alternative in the event other nominating procedures fail. And a few of them use this method exclusively.

A bylaw typical of those providing for nominations from the floor is set out below.

> The Directors shall be nominated from the floor at the annual membership meeting and shall be elected by the members in attendance at such meeting.

The nomination of candidates from the floor is a democratic and simple procedure. From the standpoint of expediency, this method leaves little to be desired. However, such nominations have a spur-of-the-moment quality to them, being spontaneous and impromptu choices of one or more individual members. Unfortunately, this method sometimes results in the selection of candidates who are not sufficiently qualified as directors. It is a procedure that simply does not provide sufficient time to identify those nominees with the best qualifications, and can lead to the embarrassment of having the nominee refuse the candidacy.

The problem is compounded by the fact that some organizations have such an extensive membership and serve such a large territory that few of the members know each other well enough to judge their ability to serve as directors. Under such circumstances, the members know little, if anything, about the qualifications of the nominees they are asked to vote for. There is no chance to inform the membership in advance of the meeting, and very little opportunity to advise them on this score at the annual meeting itself.

Sec. 64. Nominations by Committee

Membership organizations frequently use nominating committees to obtain nominations to fill vacancies in elective offices.

The use of a nominating committee in the selection of candidates has many advantages, the primary one being that the committee will have time to check and carefully weigh the qualifications of each possible candidate. And where there are different and identifiable factions within the organization, or where different areas are represented, the committee method makes it possible to present an evenly balanced slate from among the various groups or areas. Finally, each prospective candidate can be interviewed in advance to determine his willingness to serve if elected.

Particularly advantageous, in the nominating committee system, is the fact that the choices of the committee can be publicized in advance of the annual meeting. An appropriate notice can be circulated to the membership showing the experience and qualifications of each selection. This gives the membership a chance to evaluate the candidates thoroughly, an opportunity they do not have under most other nominating methods.

If nominations are to be made by a nominating committee, the committee should be appointed far enough in advance of the election to give time for careful and wise selection of nominees, with due consideration to geographic representation.

The nominating committee should be relatively large and broadly representative of the entire membership. This tends to avoid criticism of the committee that the election is being "engineered."

The nominating committee should select at least two, and preferably three, strong nominees for each vacancy. This gives the membership a greater freedom of choice and will tend to dispel any suspicion that the election is being "railroaded."

The bylaw set out below illustrates the nominating committee method.

> At its annual meeting the membership may elect for the next election district meeting a nominating committee consisting of not less than six (6) nor more than ten (10) members who shall be members of this organization, whose duty it shall be, prior to such next election district meeting, to nominate two (2) or more persons to serve as Director and to advise delegates in the district prior to such election district meeting the names and qualifications of such nominees. In the event any member of a nominating committee shall be unable or unwilling to serve, the remaining members, so long as they shall not be less than four (4) in number, shall have full power to act.

Under such a bylaw, any member in good standing is eligible to serve on the nominating committee.

It should be noted, in concluding the discussion of this method of nominating candidates, that the use of a nominating committee ordinarily does not, and should not, preclude the possibility of other nominations from the floor.

Sec. 65. Nominations by Petition

One plan for the selection of candidates for directors is that of nomination by petition of the membership in advance of the annual meeting. This method requires that the members themselves take the initiative in selecting candidates. A typical bylaw providing for the nomination of directors by petition is set out below.

> Nominations for Directors, either at large or for a district, shall be made by petition addressed to the Secretary, requesting him to place on the ballot the name of the person so nominated. Such a petition shall be signed by not less than twenty (20) members and shall be filed with the Secretary not less than twenty (20) nor more than sixty (60) days before the annual meeting of the membership. The Secretary will promptly examine the petition, the signatures thereto, and determine the eligibility of the nominee

and the signers, and if he finds it in compliance with the bylaws, he shall endorse thereon his signed statement to that effect. The person or persons so nominated shall be the candidate or candidates to be voted on as hereinafter provided.

The procedure calling for the nomination of candidates for director by petition is not always reliable. It is dependent upon the membership putting forth the time and effort necessary to get the required number of signatures to their petitions. If they are unsuccessful in obtaining signatures, the entire plan fails. In addition, there may simply be insufficient interest on the part of the membership in choosing directors as their representatives.

Sec. 66. Nominations by District Caucus

Many membership organizations provide for nominations of directors by district caucus at the annual membership meeting. The plan for district caucus nominations should be set forth in a bylaw, such as the one set out below.

> At each annual meeting, voting delegates or representatives of members in good standing shall caucus by districts as hereinabove established and present to the annual meeting following such district caucuses the names of not more than two (2) candidates for Director from each district wherein a vacancy exists. In the event a district caucus shall unanimously agree upon a single nominee for Director, the name of such nominee shall alone be submitted to the membership.

Any plan for the nomination of candidates for director by district caucus usually requires that the chairman designate separate rooms or locations where the members in attendance from each district are to meet and caucus. The chairman may appoint a leader from the members of each district to conduct the district caucus nomination meetings and report the nominations back to the general membership. The membership then hears the nominations and elects a slate of directors.

Frequently, only one name from each district is submitted to the membership for election or confirmation. This may occur because that name was the only name placed in nomination. Or it may occur because the nomination vote is by voice, and this method of voting seldom leads to more than one nomination.

The procedure for nomination of candidates for director by

district caucus at the annual meeting is not recommended. This procedure permits little, if any, advance planning. Most members have no concept as to who they will support for director in advance of the annual meeting. And they have no chance to familiarize themselves with the background and experience of each candidate. Hence a district caucus does not always produce the strongest candidates available. Furthermore, remote districts are apt to be poorly represented at the annual meeting, in which case there may be some difficulty in arriving at a strong, well-qualified candidate.

Sec. 67. Nominations by District Primary

Under the district primary system, two—or possibly more —persons are nominated from each district as candidates for a seat on the board of directors. Subsequently, usually at the annual meeting, a runoff election is held to determine which candidate is to be elected to sit on the board.

A few organizations both nominate and elect their directors at district meetings. Ordinarily, however, the bylaws should provide only for nomination at district meetings, with elections or confirmation taking place at the annual meeting.

Any plan for director nominations by districts requires that the territory served by the organization be divided into director districts and that one or more directors be nominated by members residing in each district. As a rule, such nominations are made in district membership meetings held prior to the annual meeting. However, they may also be made at annual membership meetings by dividing the membership in attendance into districts. In this regard, the bylaws will frequently specify the districts by boundaries or define them in some other way. If so, the bylaws should also specify redistricting procedures to be followed in case the districts become unbalanced from the standpoint of membership representation.

The district primary system is intended to ensure that members be more directly represented on the board and to make certain that the board will be decentralized and diversified. The so-called district system has the advantage of making it easier for members to take an active and direct part in the affairs of the organization.

District nomination meetings have the effect of bringing the organization closer to its membership and generally provide an effective system for the selection of directors. The system is especially well suited to organizations that serve a large territory, for the plan ensures distribution of, and representation by, the directors over a large geographical area. Such a plan is administratively more difficult, of course, since schedules must be prepared and notice must be given of all of the various meetings.

Organizations whose bylaws provide for the nomination of directors at district meetings should permit the nomination of other candidates from the floor at the annual membership meeting, although any candidate so nominated should reside in the same district as the candidate he is opposing.

The bylaws of federated organizations often specify that nominees for directors at the regional level will be made by member associations. In such cases, nomination by member associations is equivalent to nomination by districts, since the nominees chosen are selected from the territory in which the member association operates.

A typical bylaw providing for nomination of directors through district primaries is set out below.

> The members of each district shall be called together thirty (30) days prior to the annual meeting of all members. Where there will be a vacancy at such ensuing annual meeting, the district shall select one (1) member as a nominee for the Association's Board of Directors. Such nominee must reside within the district holding the nomination election. Such nominee shall be presented for election at the ensuing annual meeting of all members.

Another version of a bylaw providing for nomination of candidates for director vacancies by districts is set out below.

> At least fifteen (15) days prior to the annual meeting at which the term of a Director of any district shall expire, a primary election shall be held in such district for the purpose of electing a Director for such district for the next term, and all members in such district shall be entitled to participate in such election. Directors elected in the respective districts shall be deemed thereby elected as Directors of this organization and shall, if qualified, be accepted and elected at the regular meeting of this organization and thereupon admitted to Board membership.

Redistricting Procedure

The bylaws should make provisions for redistricting procedures in the event the districts become unbalanced from the standpoint of membership representation. Redistricting may be brought about by action of the directors, by vote of the membership, or through a redistricting committee. Whatever plan is adopted, it should be made mandatory and specified in the bylaws, particularly where the plan is to be implemented by action of the board. Where redistricting is left to the discretion of the directors, they are reluctant to act because they are involved in decisions affecting their own offices.

The bylaw set out below is typical of redistricting provisions that give the necessary mandate to the board of directors.

> Prior to the tenth day of July of each year, the Board shall review the districts as hereinbefore defined and ascertain whether or not such districts as delineated and the number of Directors allotted to each constitute fair and equitable district representation. Should the Board find that any of said districts do not properly reflect fair and equitable district representation, the Board shall reapportion the number of Directors, or redistrict the territory covered by this organization, or both, after thirty (30) days' written notice to all members of this organization of the proposed action.

Another, somewhat simpler, redistricting bylaw gives the necessary authority to a special committee; it is set out below.

> Whenever changes in district boundaries seem desirable, the Board of Directors shall appoint one (1) Director and two (2) members resident in each district as then constituted to a rezoning or redistricting commission. At the request of the Directors, the persons comprising such a commission shall meet on ten (10) days' notice by mail to consider desirable changes and prepare a report. A majority of the members of the commission shall constitute a quorum at commission meetings.

Where the bylaws provide for a redistricting committee, the majority thereof should be composed of persons who are not members of the board of directors. This tends to assure more objectivity than where redistricting is left entirely to directors.

Sec. 68. Nominations by Mail

A little-used method of nominating directors is to provide for nominations from the membership by mail. In organizations with a small membership and operating in a limited area, the mail nomination system has certain advantages. The process is essentially a democratic one, with each member being given a chance to place in nomination anyone he feels qualified to assume the responsibility of director. And members need not attend the annual meeting to participate in the process. However, in those organizations with large memberships, the method tends to become cumbersome and impracticable, involving much paper work and a relatively large administrative staff.

A bylaw typical of those providing for mail nominations is set out below.

> Not less than forty (40) days prior to the annual meeting, the Secretary shall mail to each member a list of all the members eligible to vote within his district as of January 1 immediately preceding the annual meeting for which the election is being conducted. The Secretary shall further include with such list a ballot with instructions for the member to designate his preference for a candidate or candidates, as the case may be, from said list, to fill any vacancy on the Board of Directors. Each member shall be entitled to vote for that number of candidates equal to the number of Directorships to be filled for his district. The Secretary shall further include a notice for the last date for receiving such ballots.

Sec. 69. Nominations in Federated Organizations

Federated membership organizations generally secure nominations for directorships from member associations. The bylaws may provide either that the nominations for directors are to be made by the local association memberships or that the board of directors of the member associations are to make the director nominations for the parent body.

Under still another plan, nomination for director at the member association level is equivalent to election to the national or regional board. Under such a plan, the election of directors at the annual meeting of the national or regional organization consists of the confirmation of the nominees designated by member associations.

Some federated organizations leave the method of selecting officers for the board of the parent body to the discretion of the local member associations. The bylaw of such an organization might simply declare:

> Each local association shall be entitled to designate two (2) persons to represent it upon the regional board.

Where directors of regional associations are nominated and

elected by districts, the bylaws generally require that the directors reside in the district from which they are nominated. Some federated regional associations narrow the field still further by requiring that directors must be directors of a member association. Still others specify that the director elected to the board of a federated association must be a manager, director, or employee of a member association. The bylaw set out below is representative.

> Only persons who are members of the Board of Directors or are officers or employees of a regional association having membership in this Association shall be eligible for election to the Board of Directors of this Association.

Sec. 70. Handling Nominations in Meetings

The presentation of nominations at a meeting are initiated by the presiding officer, who says, "Nominations for the office of [TITLE OF OFFICE] are now in order." If a nominating committee system is being used, the presiding officer should call for the committee report at the appropriate time. The report of this committee constitutes the official nomination of those persons named in the report for the offices to be filled.

The presiding officer, following the presentation of the report of the nominating committee, may then ask for further nominations for each office in turn from the floor and add these names to those names listed in the committee report.

If a nominating committee is not used, all nominations for offices should come from the membership. Any member may rise to make a nomination from the floor. Such nominations do not require a second. Upon being recognized by the presiding officer, the member says, "I nominate [NAME OF MEMBER] for [TITLE OF OFFICE]."

The presiding officer should repeat the names of persons nominated from the floor and may ask the person nominated to stand so as to make certain that all concerned know who is being nominated. The recording secretary should keep a special record of all nominations.

The nominations should be closed by the presiding officer when it becomes apparent that no further nominations for a particular office are to be made. He does this by saying, "Are there any other nominations for the office of [TITLE OF OFFICE]?" If there is no response to this request, he should declare that nominations for that office are closed.

—⑨—

ELECTION
VOTING
METHODS

Sec. 71. Kinds of Voting Methods

Members vote for the officers and directors of their organizations in several different ways. The most common are (1) by acclamation, (2) by direct ballot, (3) by mail ballot, (4) by proxy voting, and (5) by cumulative voting.

In some organizations a combination of two or more methods of voting is permitted. For example, the members may cast their votes for directors in person, or they may vote by mail where the bylaws so permit. Similarly, an organization may permit both direct balloting and balloting through proxy (not recommended) or by cumulative voting. (See Sec. 74 *infra*.)

Many membership organizations not only nominate their directors at district primaries (see Sec. 67 *supra*) but use the same or similar procedure in holding runoff elections at the annual meeting. That is, the vote is by district in determining who is to sit on the board. In other associations or organizations the membership of a particular district will at the annual meeting vote to confirm an election held at the district level.

Another system used by organizations with large memberships spread over a wide area is that of balloting by delegates. In an election for a seat on the board, for example, the ballot of one delegate may represent the vote of fifty or a hundred or two hundred or more individual members. Ideally, under such a procedure, each delegate may cast as many votes at any meeting as the members of the group represented by him could cast if present at the meeting.

An election will not be overturned for a voting irregularity unless the irregularity is such as to affect the outcome of the election. A mere mistake in the number of ballot boxes maintained, for example, would not affect the outcome of the election and would not be regarded as a sufficient basis for overturning the election. (1 Hinds' Precedents[1] Sec. 456.)

Sec. 72. Voting by Acclamation; *Viva Voce* Procedures

The election of the various officers of the organization, such as the clerk and doorkeeper, may be by *viva voce*, or voice vote. (1 HP Sec. 81.) Such votes are taken pursuant to either formal or informal procedures. Under the formal procedure, the clerk appoints tellers who make a record as each member, when the roll is called, announces the name of the candidate of his choice. The teller then announces the number of votes that have been received by each candidate. (1 HP Sec. 81.) The clerk, after restating the reported vote, announces that: "Mr. [NAME OF CANDIDATE], having received the majority of all the votes cast, is duly elected chairman of [NAME OF ORGANIZATION]."

Voting by informal acclamation—that is, where all the members collectively shout their votes for or against a particular candidate—may be used where one of the candidates has little or no opposition. But it is not recommended for all elections nor for all types of membership organizations. More often than not, in closely contested elections, such votes do not reflect the real wishes of the membership. Such votes are often based on emotional considerations, with the silent opposition vote going unrecorded. Nevertheless, voting by acclamation is an acknowledged time-saver and is still the procedure used by many membership organizations, particularly smaller and less well organized ones. It may be provided for in the bylaws, with close contests excepted, as follows:

> The voting at all meetings may be *viva voce* but forty (40) percent of those present as determined by the Presiding Officer may demand a vote by secret ballot, whereupon such vote shall be taken.

In the bylaw quoted above, when members vote by voice it is a one-member-one-vote election. However, a bylaw providing for voting by acclamation may include an alternative procedure by which proportional voting is permitted.

[1] Hereinafter cited as HP.

Sec. 73. Voting by Ballot

One of the best methods of voting for the directors and other officers is by written ballot, which need not be signed or otherwise identified. This enables the member to vote privately, avoids irrelevant pressures, and frees him from the possible embarrassment of having voted publicly against a friend or for the losing candidate.

A bylaw typical of those providing for the ballot method of voting is as follows:

> Except as may be suspended at any meeting by the unanimous action of those present and entitled to vote, all elections shall be by ballot.

Where ballots are to be used in the elections for officers and directors, the ballots should show the nominees' names and provide additional space for the names of "write-in" candidates. If considered desirable, especially in large organizations, ballots may be accompanied by short biographical statements regarding each candidate. Such organizations might also find it advantageous to publish the names and qualifications of the candidates, with photographs, in the organization's newsletter or other publications that precede the election.

The ballots should be distributed and counted by a tellers' committee. This committee should be given the responsibility of seeing that the voting is conducted in accordance with the bylaws. When counted, the ballots should be turned over to the secretary or the recording officer of the organization, who should be instructed to preserve the ballots for a reasonable time.

Sec. 74. Cumulative Voting

Cumulative voting is a system of voting by which each member is given a number of votes equal to the number of officers or directors to be chosen, and who is allowed to concentrate the whole number of his votes on one person, or to distribute them as he sees fit. For example, if four directors of an organization are to be elected, then, under this system, the voter may cast four votes for one person, or two votes for each of two persons, or he may cast three votes for one person and one vote for another person. Cumulative voting is intended to secure larger representation on behalf of a minority.

In essence, cumulative voting permits a member to concentrate the full force of his vote behind one candidate if he so chooses.

A bylaw typical of those providing for cumulative voting is set out below.

> Every member shall have the right to vote for as many persons as there are Directors to be elected, or to cumulate said votes so as to give them all to one candidate or to distribute them among as many candidates as he shall see fit.

Sec. 75. Majority Votes; Plurality Votes Distinguished

A simple majority vote is required for the election of officers. This is the rule in the U.S. House of Representatives (6 Cannon's Precedents[2] Sec. 23) and in most membership organizations. And it is not necessary to the validity of the election of a chairman that he receive a majority of the votes of *all* members. It is sufficient that he receive a majority of the votes of those present. In 1890 the requirement in the House of Representatives that a quorum actually vote was dropped in favor of the requirement that a quorum be merely present. Thus, an election of the Speaker is valid even though he receives merely a majority of votes of those present, provided that a quorum is in fact present. (1 HP Sec. 216.)

Accordingly, it is the general rule that a majority of all votes cast is necessary to elect a nominee to office, unless otherwise provided for in the bylaws. If no single candidate obtains such a majority, which can happen if there are several candidates for one office, then the vote must be taken over again. It is possible, in this situation, to go through the voting procedure a number of times with no single candidate ever obtaining a majority. To avoid this problem, the organization might require the withdrawal of the candidate with the smallest number of votes at each successive balloting.

If the organization finds that this withdrawal and runoff system is unwieldy and time-consuming, as it generally is, it may alter its bylaws to provide that a plurality of votes, rather than a majority of votes, is sufficient to elect. Under the plurality system, a candidate with a greater number of votes than any other candidate is deemed elected, even though he does not receive a majority of the total votes cast.

When a candidate is elected pursuant to a plurality, it is advisable for his election to be confirmed by a simple majority.

If there is not sufficient time to amend the bylaws, then it may

[2] Hereinafter cited as CP.

be possible to achieve the same objective by special resolution. Often, the membership may by special resolution adopt a rule that will authorize the election of officers by a plurality. Such a rule permits the election of a candidate who has received more votes than any other candidate, though his total may be far less than a majority. (1 HP Secs. 221, 222.)

–10–

MEMBERS

Sec. 76. Rights of Membership; Ownership and Control

In the final analysis, ultimate control over the affairs of an organization is vested in the members. The membership creates the organization, and it has the power to drastically alter its course or even, subject to its charter and bylaws, terminate it.

The powers that the members have in controlling the organization must be exercised democratically. In general, every member of an organization has equal rights and privileges. Each knows that his vote will carry just as much weight as that of any other member. And although every member may not be permitted to speak on every issue, his views can be made known through a designated leader, whether for the majority or minority.

The members have a right to approve fundamental policies of the highest importance in the management of the organization. They have the right to adopt bylaws or changes therein, and they have the right to approve or disapprove of such matters as a merger or a consolidation with another organization, credit extensions, adoption of a retirement system for employees, and changes in the financial structure of the organization. Examples of policy determinations that should be submitted to the membership include (1) a major expansion in the facilities of the organization, (2) changes in capital structure, and (3) a major change in the kind of services offered to the membership.

In exercising their right to control policy, the members may:

1. Offer motions and resolutions relating to the affairs of the organization.
2. Elect and remove directors.
3. Receive and pass on reports of officers and committees.
4. Adopt and amend bylaws.
5. Approve changes in the capital structure of the organization.
6. Approve loans under certain circumstances.

149

7.   Require officers, directors, and other agents of the organization to comply with the charter or the bylaws.

8.   Take legal action to hold directors and officers liable for their failure to comply with the charter or bylaws.

9.   Examine the organization's books, records, and property, subject to reasonable restrictions.

As noted above, it is ordinarily a member's right to participate in the selection of a competent board of directors. This right stems from the fact that although the members have the ultimate right of control, they cannot make all decisions directly, and so must elect directors to represent them in various affairs of management. Moreover, since the competency of the board depends on the wisdom and judgment of the members in electing directors, the members should understand and evaluate board actions and stand ready to remove any directors who are not carrying out the duties entrusted to them.

Sec. 77. Right to Membership

As a matter of general principle, every deliberative body is said to have unlimited control over the qualifications or disqualifications of its members, except as specifically limited by organic law. (1 Hinds' Precedents[1] Sec. 477.) Indeed, historically, organization membership has been considered a privilege that may be withheld or granted at will.[2]

However, there are limitations on the power of legislative organizations to exclude members who have been duly elected by their constituents. The U.S. Supreme Court has held that because the Constitution grants authority to the House of Representatives to judge the qualifications of its members only with respect to age, citizenship, and inhabitancy, any attempt by the House to attach additional qualifications to a member-elect is subject to judicial review. Moreover, in judging the qualifications of its members, Congress is limited to the standing qualifications prescribed in the Constitution, and the House is without power to exclude a member on other grounds.[3]

[1] Hereinafter cited as HP.

[2] See *Medical Society of Mobile County* v. *Walker*, 245 Ala. 135, 16 So. 2d 321 (1944).

[3] *Powell* v. *McCormack*, 395 U.S. 486 (1969).

Exceptions to the concept of organizational autonomy have also been recognized in the area of civil and property rights.[4] For example, where membership in a professional society is a virtual prerequisite to the practice of the particular profession, the courts will scrutinize the organization's membership standards and screening procedures notwithstanding their recognition of the fact that professional societies possess a specialized competence in evaluating the qualifications of an individual to engage in professional activities.[5]

The acceptance or rejection of membership applications is also subject to special rules in those cases where the organization is a trade association. Under the antitrust laws, business competitors may not be excluded from membership in an organization if the exclusion would unreasonably restrict competitive opportunities in the industry. Whether exclusion will have this effect depends on many factors, including the economic advantages afforded by the organization to members, the nature of the industry, and the type of business conducted by the particular applicant. Thus, a bylaw of a trade association may be held invalid if it empowers association members to arbitrarily prevent business competitors from becoming members.[6]

A trade association may prescribe in its bylaws some method of screening membership applicants to ensure that the applicant is actually in the industry or segment thereof with which the association is concerned. However, the screening system should not be used as a device for excluding bona fide competitors.

A difficult question arises where a trade association denies a membership application because of alleged unethical business conduct. However, the ethical grounds should be clear and not based solely on aggressive competitive practices, such as price-cutting. Indeed, the denial of membership because of price-cutting should be avoided, as this may suggest a possible antitrust law violation on the part of the association. Moreover, great care should be exercised as to the manner of excluding such an applicant so as to avoid any taint of libel or slander on the part of the association.

Nonlegislative membership organizations must consider the

[4]*S.T.P. Corp.* v. *United States Auto Club, Inc.*, 286 F. Supp. 146 (1968).

[5]*Marjorie Webster Junior College, Inc.*, v. *Middle States Ass'n of Colleges & Secondary Schools, Inc.*, 432 F. 2d 650 (1970).

[6]Cf. *Montague & Co.* v. *Lowry*, 193 U.S. 38 (1904).

application of the Civil Rights Act of 1964, especially the public accommodations title of that statute, which secures equal access to and equal treatment in places of public accommodation. Under this statute, the Attorney General may bring a civil action for "such preventative relief, including an application for a permanent or temporary injunction . . ." whenever he has "reasonable cause to believe that any person or group of persons is engaged in a pattern or practice of resistance to the full enjoyment of any of the rights secured by" the statute.

When Congress passed this legislation, it included, among other exceptions, a provision that the act should not apply to a private club or other establishment not in fact open to the public. (42 U.S. Code Sec. 2000 a (e).) In construing this statute, the courts have tended to distinguish between truly private clubs and those that are not in fact private, and in so doing have emphasized the importance of various characteristics that most private clubs generally possess.

In making this distinction, the courts have been influenced by such factors as whether or not the membership is genuinely selective and whether or not the members have any control over the club's operations. The more selective a club's membership is, the more likely it is that the club is a private rather than a public accommodation. Thus, the fact that the members have no right to vote on whether applicants should be accepted as new members has led the courts to conclude that the organizations involved were not private.[7]

Another factor to be considered in determining the question of whether the club is genuinely selective is whether the members have any control over the revocation of a membership.[8] Similarly, a club with no limits on its membership and with no articulated standards for admission may be considered too unselective in its policies to be adjudicated a private club.[9]

The courts have also considered the number of members in relation to the population and area from which members could be drawn. Thus, a restaurant club that had more than 21,000 members, only one of whom was a Negro, and that charged a lifetime admission fee of ten cents, was held not to be a private club.[10]

[7]See *Bell* v. *Kenwood Golf and Country Club, Inc.* (1970, DC, Md.) 314 F. Supp. 753; *Wright* v. *Cork Club* (1970, DC, Tex.) 315 F. Supp. 1143.

[8]*U.S.* v. *Johnson Lake, Inc.* (1970, DC, Ala.) 312 F. Supp. 1376.

[9]*Nesmith* v. *YMCA*, 397 F. 2d 96.

[10]*Bradshaw* v. *Whigam*, 11 Race Rel L Rep 934.

Another restaurant was held not to be a private club where it appeared that it had 12,000 members, 2,400 of whom would have had to be present in person or by proxy in order to constitute a quorum that could alter or repeal a bylaw adopted by the board of trustees, which consisted of the restaurant's owner and his wife and daughter.[11]

Sec. 78. Membership Qualifications

The qualifications that must be possessed by a person in order to be eligible for membership in an organization are generally provided for in its constitution or bylaws or both. They may provide, for example, that a member must be in a certain line of business, or reside in a certain area, or be of a certain age and citizenship. In drafting such provisions, organizers should bear in mind that if the constitution spells out the qualifications, they cannot be changed except by an amendment of the constitution.

Those provisions of the bylaws or constitution that set forth the qualifications of or for membership should be drawn with great care. The requirements of membership should be stated affirmatively and in the clearest possible language, so as to avoid the contention that a person is eligible to a seat if only because he is not expressly disqualified by the constitution. (1 IIP Sec. 442.) In this respect, if the listing of qualifications in the bylaws or constitution is affirmatively stated, the argument may be made that the list of qualifications is intended to be exclusive. But if the constitutional provision or bylaw merely enumerates a few disqualifications, and states them in the negative, the organization may impose additional ones not enumerated therein. (1 HP Sec. 477.)

So far as legislative organizations are concerned, as has already been noted, the U.S. Supreme Court has ruled that Congress, in judging the qualifications of its members, is limited to the standing qualifications prescribed in the Constitution, and that the House of Representatives may not in excluding a member look to other qualifications not specified therein.[12]

Although the qualifications of membership should be specified in the bylaws, these qualifications should be broadly defined and be coupled with a provision giving the board of directors full discretion and wide powers in determining the admission of applicants to membership. If membership is defined too narrowly, it

[11]*U.S. by Katzenbach v. Jack Sabin's Private Club*, 265 F. Supp. 90.

[12]*Powell v. McCormack*, 395 U.S. 486 (1969).

will hinder the organization's growth and limit the effectiveness of its activities. It is most important that the board have discretionary powers in this respect.

The bylaw dealing with membership may limit membership to those persons having interests that coincide with those of the organization; for example, the bylaws may limit membership to those who participate in certain occupations or professions, distribute certain merchandise, deal in a specified service, or manufacture a particular product. Moreover, the organization may limit its membership still further by focusing on a particular level of an industry or a profession. Thus, a bylaw may limit membership to wholesalers of a particular product, or may limit membership to a combination of industry levels, as illustrated in the bylaw below.

> Any person, firm, or corporation engaged in the sale of automobiles as a dealer, retailer, distributor, or jobber is eligible to become a regular member.

A specified number of years of experience in a particular profession or business is also a legitimate membership requirement. For example, the Professional Golfers Association requires that prospective members show five years of professional golfing experience before being accepted for competition in its authorized golfing events, and such bylaws have been upheld by the courts.[13]

Membership may be divided into various classes, such as active, associate, and honorary members. This arrangement is most common among professional membership organizations. Other organizations have such categories as "affiliate" memberships, which may be limited to enrolled students or other persons with limited qualifications. Thus, the American Society of Landscape Architects divides its membership into the following categories:

> *Member.* Open to landscape architects at least twenty-seven years of age and having five years of experience.
>
> *Fellow.* Open to those having ten years' standing as members.
>
> *Corresponding member.* Open to distinguished foreign landscape architects.
>
> *Honorary member.* Open to those performing notable service in advancing the cause of landscape architecture.
>
> *Affiliate.* Open to enrolled students or persons holding a degree in landscape architecture from an accredited educational institution.

Most membership organizations also limit the territory from

---

[13]*Deesen* v. *Professional Golfers Association of America*, 358 F. 2d 165 (1966).

which members are drawn. The size of the territory depends in large measure upon the nature of the organization and the services it seeks to provide. Obviously, the territory should be no larger than will permit efficient service to the members.

Sec. 79. Holding Incompatible Office as Disqualification

The charter or bylaws of a membership organization may declare the holding of certain offices outside the organization to be incompatible with membership. Under such a provision, a member may be deemed to have disqualified himself by the holding of such an office. (1 HP Sec. 492.) He cannot simultaneously claim his right to a seat as a member at the same time that he holds the proscribed incompatible office. He may resign the incompatible office, of course, but unless he does so the membership may declare his seat as a member to be vacant. (1 HP Secs. 492-98.)

Incompatibility will be deemed to exist where the nature and duties of the two offices are such as to render it improper, from policy considerations, for one incumbent to fill both, the rule being that the acceptance of the second office vacates the first. (6 Cannon's Precedents[14] Sec. 60.) However, he may hold both offices until such time as he is required to take his seat as a member, and if that seat is contested, he may postpone making a choice between them until such time as the membership resolves the question pertaining to his seat. (1 HP Sec. 505.)

The question as to whether or not two offices are incompatible is generally a factual one, which may be referred to a committee for an investigation and report. (6 CP Sec. 62.) A resolution directing such an investigation may take the following form:

> *Resolved*, That the Membership Committee be instructed to ascertain and report to the membership whether any member is at present holding an office in [NAME OF OFFICE OR ORGANIZATION], and whether the holding of such office vacates the seat of such member. [6 CP Sec. 62.]

Such a resolution is privileged. (6 CP Sec. 62.)

Sec. 80. Determining Eligibility; Procedure

All membership organizations should have some established procedure for ascertaining or investigating the qualifications or cre-

---

[14]Hereinafter cited as CP.

dentials of its members. (1 HP Secs. 528-88.) Frequently, as already pointed out, the board of directors is given discretionary powers to resolve questions concerning the qualification of a member or an applicant for membership. (See Sec. 78 *supra*.) Questions concerning qualifications may also be referred to a committee. (1 HP Sec. 136.) But the constitution or bylaws will often provide that the membership itself has the authority to judge or determine the qualifications of its members. In this event, questions concerning the qualifications of an individual to participate as a member are to be resolved by the membership, not the presiding officer. (1 HP Sec. 135.)

Whatever procedure is used, in each case the applicant's eligibility for membership should be determined by measuring his qualifications against the statements in the organizing documents defining the interests with which the organization is concerned and setting forth the goals that are its objectives. These statements are generally found in the organization's statement of purpose or in those provisions that prescribe the qualifications or requirements for membership. (See Secs. 32-44 *supra*.)

Questions regarding the qualifications of an individual may be resolved by the membership itself, for an organization always has the right to correct the roll of qualified members. It may add to or strike from this roll. Questions as to qualifications may be debated by the members, and votes may be taken on whether an individual is in fact qualified. (1 HP Secs. 19-21.) Thus, when the right of a member to participate is challenged, motions and debate thereon are in order. Such a challenge raises a question of the highest privilege, although other business may intervene by unanimous consent. (1 HP Secs. 149-54.) It follows that when a resolution pertaining to a member's right to a seat is brought before the membership independently of a committee, a question of privilege is raised, and the proponent's right to prior recognition for debate takes precedence over the motion to refer to committee. (6 CP Sec. 86.)

Whether a particular individual is in fact qualified may be put to a vote of the full membership pursuant to a resolution such as the following:

> *Resolved*, That Mr. [NAME OF MEMBER], who has presented documents claiming to represent the [NAME OF DISTRICT], is not entitled to a seat, and that such seat is vacant. [1 HP Sec. 415.]

Likewise, the membership may, by a majority vote, unseat a

member who does not possess the required qualifications. (1 HP Sec. 428.)

When a resolution pertaining to the right of a member to a seat is proposed, the membership may refer the matter to committee for immediate consideration or vote to table the resolution. A motion to table in such a case takes precedence over a motion to refer to committee. (6 CP Sec. 86.)

A special committee may be established to resolve questions regarding the credentials of one or more members. (1 HP Sec. 16.) In some organizations the member whose qualifications are questioned is permitted to be present before the committee, to cross-examine witnesses, and to offer evidence. (1 HP Sec. 420.) After the committee has investigated the matter, it reports on the facts to the full membership, usually with its recommendations. (1 HP Secs. 528-733.)

A person whose credentials are not in order, or who is otherwise unqualified, should be excluded by the clerk in preparing the roll of participating members. (1 HP Sec. 14.) An organization may repudiate the action of a clerk in enrolling a person whose credentials are not in order. (1 HP Sec. 53.) Thus, a person whose credentials are lost should not be seated until it is clearly shown that his qualifications are in no way disputed. (1 HP Sec. 85.) Where there is no question as to the qualifications of a particular member, however, he may be seated by unanimous consent even though his credentials are not immediately available. (1 HP Sec. 81.)

In determining whether the credentials of an individual are in order, the test should be whether they are in substantial compliance with the requirements; technical irregularities may be disregarded. (1 HP Sec. 32.) And although they may not be in a form sufficient to satisfy the clerk, the membership may deem them to be satisfactory. (1 HP Sec. 30.) However, where two persons claim the same seat, and neither can show the proper credentials, the clerk may refuse to enroll either of them. (1 HP Secs. 34-35.) In the event that it is impossible or impracticable to determine with any certainty who is entitled to the seat, the seat may be declared vacant. (1 HP Sec. 55.)

Questions concerning the qualifications of an individual to sit as a member should not be taken up until after the election of the presiding officer. During the preliminary stages of organization, the clerk's roll governs who is to be permitted to participate or be recognized. A person whose name is not on the roll should not be recognized. (1 HP Sec. 86.) In this regard, the determination of a question concerning an enrolled member's right to participate has priority over the determination of questions of challenge involving members whose names do not appear on the clerk's roll. (1 HP Sec. 155.) And the fact that a particular member has not yet been seated does not prevent him from challenging the right of another member to participate. (1 HP Sec. 141.) Nor is the right to vote on such questions confined to those already seated. (1 HP Sec. 142.) The presiding officer may permit the participation of a person whose credentials are in order and regular in form, even though that person's seat is seriously disputed. However, the membership may reverse the decision of the chairman in this respect; or it may permit such a person to vote on a question and subsequently decide that his vote shall not be counted. (1 HP Sec. 103.)

In the absence of some provision in the bylaws to the contrary, a member is not to be deemed disqualified merely because he fails to appear and participate until several months after the membership has been organized. (1 HP Sec. 161.)

Sec. 81. Roll of Members

One of the duties of the clerk or secretary of a membership organization is to establish and maintain a roll of members who are qualified to participate in the affairs of the organization. (1 HP Sec. 14.) In most membership organizations this roll is made up just before the annual meeting of the organization, at which time the clerk enrolls such members as are shown by his records to be members in good standing. If the circumstances are such that he cannot perform this duty, it devolves to the sergeant at arms and then to the doorkeeper. (1 HP Sec. 253.)

Minor errors in the roll may be corrected by the clerk after examination of credentials or other papers, even in the absence of a motion instructing him to do so. (1 HP Sec. 25.) The clerk has the duty of keeping this roll up to date and must take notice of any deaths or resignations among the membership. Deletions made from the roll by the clerk should be brought to the attention of the membership from time to time. (1 HP Sec. 26.)

The initiative in correcting the roll may come from someone whose name has been incorrectly included thereon. In such a case, he may simply ask the clerk to delete his name from the roll. (1 HP Sec. 29.)

Sec. 82. Membership Relations

All successful membership organizations have a sound membership relations program. In developing such programs, an organization must be sensitive to the desires of all of its members, not just a few. This is essential because all members have voting rights and because participation on the part of any member is voluntary. If certain members are given preferential treatment, the others are likely to be unwilling to participate. Membership participation creates interest, enthusiasm, and loyalty that cannot be achieved in any other way.

A constant flow of information is the mainspring that drives a good membership program. First, there must be a flow of information from the organization to its members; second, members must have an opportunity to convey their wants and opinions to the organization. In other words, there must be a means for each to initiate the flow of information as well as to react to information received.

Every member should clearly understand what membership in his organization means—why members join, how they benefit, and what obligations they assume. A member should also be well informed concerning the functions and operations of his organization—its current status and prospects for the future. He should be fully informed as to the history of his organization in general, its goals, and how it differs from other, perhaps similar, organizations. The organization has the responsibility to make this information available to every member either before he joins or soon thereafter.

There is no doubt that every member should also be familiar with the basic documents of his organization. He can determine from the bylaws provided to him how he as a member is represented by the board of directors, how elections are conducted, and how he benefits along with other members. Articles of incorporation, rules of order, and policy resolutions are among the other documents that should be supplied to each member and that each member should feel obligated to study.

Since the financial condition of their organization is a matter of concern to all members, they should, at regular intervals, be supplied with operating statements and balance sheets.

As a rule, reports to the membership from committee chairmen, directors, and management should contain basic information and should be presented in the form that the average member will readily comprehend. Frequently, they can be presented as summaries. Reports concerning the adoption of new policies or changes in existing policies should be communicated to the membership.

Where reports are to be presented at the membership meeting, it is good practice to permit them to be followed by a question-and-answer period. Members then may ask for further details if they feel that the information was presented in a form that was too condensed. Similarly, when reports are mailed out to members, they should include a notation, where appropriate, that additional information may be supplied on request.

There is a limit, however, to the extent of detail that should be furnished members. And there are circumstances when the board of directors should actually withhold information. Personal information pertaining to the staff, for example, is customarily withheld from the membership at large. Although members have a right to know that employees are being paid according to a certain wage scale, as well as the total figure budgeted for salaries, the exact salary of an individual employee and information in his personnel file are considered confidential.

It should also be pointed out that under some conditions the release of full information to the general membership may be damaging to the organization. An example would be information pertaining to the negotiation of a new contract with a supplier. The details of such negotiations should not be disclosed to the membership, because there may be a few members who have a personal interest in a competitor and would not be reluctant to disclose this information.

The premature disclosure to the membership of a possible merger or consolidation can be disastrous. Proposals of this nature are highly controversial and emotional, and it is usually best to avoid discussions concerning them with members until the board of directors is ready to submit a recommendation. At that time, the board should be prepared to present to the membership full details of the action contemplated.

The purchase or sale of real estate by the organization is another matter that must often be handled quietly without widespread advance disclosure to the general membership. Experience has shown that serious problems can arise if such information is disclosed prematurely.

Sec. 83. In National Organizations

As federated membership organizations grow in size, integrate their operations, and become national in scope, the problem of maintaining good membership relations intensifies. It becomes increasingly difficult for them to preserve satisfactory lines of communications back to the individual members.

The organizational structure of a federated membership organization tends to insulate it from the very people it is supposed to serve. The case of a national cooperative whose membership is made up exclusively of other regional cooperatives is a classic example of this problem. The problem begins, at the lowest level, with the individual who is a member of his local cooperative. The local cooperative is a member of the regional cooperative. The regional cooperative is a member of a national federation of cooperatives, which functions as a trade association.

Thus, the national body, while retaining its cooperative characteristics, is isolated from the individual member from an organizational standpoint. It is for this reason that especially strong lines of communication must be built and maintained between the individual member and his national organization.

Centralized national membership organizations, which have only one set of officers, are in a position to develop healthier membership relations programs than most federated organizations. They provide shorter and clearer lines of communication from the member to his organization. Every member of a centralized organization holds direct membership in it. Every member has a vote. There are no intervening member associations with separate boards of directors standing between the member and his national organization. Ordinarily, any member in good standing is eligible to be elected to its board of directors.

Sec. 84. Expulsion or Exclusion of Members

Since every membership organization has the power to judge the qualifications of its members, it may, prior to the taking of a seat by a member, exclude him by a majority vote. It also has the power to expel a member, after he has taken his seat, but may do so only by a two-thirds vote. (1 HP Sec. 496.)[15] It is thus most important to

[15]See also U.S. Constitution, Art. I, Sec. 5.

distinguish between the procedure to *exclude* a member and the procedure to *expel* a member. A vote to declare a seat vacant is sufficiently similar to a vote to expel as to require a two-thirds vote, as distinguished from a mere majority vote, and so would justify a point of order that a resolution to declare the seat vacant is not carried if two-thirds do not vote for it. (1 HP Sec. 476.)

The distinction between expulsion and exclusion is of particular importance to legislative membership organizations. Policing the conduct of members, and possibly expelling a member for misconduct, involves different issues and different considerations quite apart from the initial decision as to whether an elected official should be seated. This distinction has been recognized by the U.S. Supreme Court, which has ruled that the U.S. House of Representatives, in excluding a member who had been duly elected by his constituents, must look to the qualifications specified in the Constitution, and may not exclude a member for disqualifications not specified therein.[16]

Subject to the requirements of the *Powell* v. *McCormack* case, every membership organization has the right to stop a member at the threshold and refuse to permit him a seat until an investigation has been made by committee as to his right thereto. Conversely, the membership may vote to permit a member to take his seat based on a prima facie showing by him, even though the question as to his qualifications is pending before a committee at the time. (1 HP Sec. 462.) Where he is seated, and his qualifications are debated at length, an agreement by the membership to a motion to table the matter has the effect of permitting the member to vote and otherwise participate in the affairs of the organization. (1 HP Sec. 461.)

The membership should refuse to entertain an objection to a person's qualifications as a member where such objection is neither supported by substantial evidence nor sustained on the personal responsibility of the objecting member. (1 HP Sec. 455.) If a specific and apparently well grounded allegation is presented, to the effect that a member-elect is not eligible, the organization may defer action in seating him until there can be an investigation as to the truth of the allegations. However, these allegations should be made by a responsible party. They should be made or vouched for

---

[16]See *Powell* v. *McCormack*, 395 U.S. 486 (1969), holding that although the House unquestionably might exercise its power to punish its members for disorderly behavior, and to expel a member with a concurrence of two-thirds, it does not have the discretionary power to deny membership by a majority vote.

by a member or officer of the organization. They should be presented at the earliest possible moment after the organizational meeting, and generally at the time the person objected to appears to claim his seat. (1 HP Sec. 474.)

In the U.S. House of Representatives, the committee to whom a question as to exclusion or expulsion is referred may receive testimony and examine witnesses under oath. This is sometimes done in the presence of the accused so that he may cross-examine the witnesses. (1 HP Sec. 475.) Such formality is generally unnecessary and inappropriate for most private membership organizations. However, the accused should always be permitted to offer at least a brief personal explanation of his choosing. (1 HP Sec. 466.) And contemporary due process requirements demand that a member of a trade association be expelled only after he has been notified of the intention to proceed against him, is given a recital of the accusation, and is accorded a fair and impartial hearing at which he may respond to the charges.[17]

Sec. 85. Grounds

The membership of a deliberative body may expel a member, by majority vote, on the ground that he lacks the necessary qualifications and is therefore ineligible. (1 HP Sec. 428.) A more difficult question is presented where a member conducts himself in a way that is detrimental to the organization, but that is not related to membership qualifications or eligibility. To provide for this eventuality, the constitution or bylaws may provide that a member may be expelled by a two-thirds vote, pursuant to specific grounds set forth therein. The bylaws may provide, for example, that a member may be suspended or terminated "for cause" upon a two-thirds vote of the board of directors.

In some organizations the constitution provides that a member may be expelled upon a two-thirds vote of the membership, but is silent as to the grounds upon which such action may be taken. Thus, in the U.S. House of Representatives, a member may be expelled from his seat by a two-thirds vote of the membership, and this may be done even though such ouster is predicated on grounds not related to the minimum qualifications for membership. (1 HP Sec. 477.) On the other hand, in excluding a member who has been

---

[17]G. D. Webster, *The Law of Associations* (Washington, D.C.: American Society of Association Executives, 1971), p. 43.

duly elected by his constituents, the House must look to the qualifications specified in the Constitution and does not have the discretionary power by majority vote to invoke a disqualification not specified therein.[18]

The power to expel a member for violating a rule of the organization is a necessary incident to the power to determine the rules of its own proceedings. The power to make rules would be nugatory unless coupled with the power to punish for disorderly behavior or disobedience to those rules. And since a member might lose all sense of dignity and disgrace the organization by his conduct, or interrupt its deliberations by violence, it has the power to expel for aggravated misconduct. But an organization should not expel a member for acts or conduct unrelated to him in his capacity as a member. (1 HP Sec. 476.)

A person otherwise entitled to a seat may be excluded as a member for acts or conduct deemed by the membership to be disloyal. (6 CP Sec. 56.) A charge of disloyalty as a basis for excluding or expelling a member may be made by another member of the organization. (1 HP Secs. 443-47.) But a member should not be expelled for disloyalty where the charges against him are not supported by sufficient evidence. (1 HP Sec. 462.) Mere suspicion of disloyalty is not sufficient to exclude a person who would otherwise be entitled to a seat. Active disloyalty must be shown by clear and satisfactory testimony. (1 HP Sec. 448.) Presumptions or suppositions alone will not suffice. (1 HP Sec. 458.) A study of the evidence by an appropriate committee is generally in order (1 HP Sec. 460), and the accused member should be permitted to take a seat pending a thorough investigation of the charge by that committee (1 HP Secs. 443-47).

Sec. 86. Criminal Conduct

A membership organization has the right to refuse to seat a person presenting himself as a member if that person has conducted himself in violation of the law. However, violations of laws that are merely directory, such as a failure to comply with technical requirements within a statutory time, although subject to civil penalties, need not be regarded as a bar to membership under extenuating circumstances. (6 CP Sec. 94.) And although an organization may exclude a member for the commission of a crime, it should not

[18]*Powell* v. *McCormack*, 395 U.S. 486 (1969).

expel him, once he has been sworn in, for an offense committed prior to his becoming a member. (6 CP Sec. 57.)

Ordinarily, a member should not be expelled for alleged crimes or immoral practices that have no connection with his duties or obligations as a member. (1 HP Sec. 470.) In fact, the mere allegation that a member has committed a crime, a conviction not having been obtained, does not give rise to a question of privilege so as to invoke the power of the organization to investigate the matter, assuming that the crime charged has no connection with his capacity to serve as a member. (1 HP Sec. 466.)

The fact that a court verdict has gone against the member is not necessarily conclusive. An appropriate committee may ignore the verdict and determine for itself any question as to the guilt or innocence of the member involved. (6 CP Sec. 56.)

Sec. 87. Resignations

In the absence of language to the contrary in the constitution or bylaws, a member may resign from the organization at any time, but should give notice thereof, either orally (2 HP Sec. 1179) or in writing (2 HP Sec. 1177). A letter tendering a resignation should be submitted to the senior officer of the organization, and may take the following form:

> To the President:
> I hereby tender my resignation as a member of [NAME OF ORGANIZATION], to take effect on [MONTH, DAY, YEAR].
> A copy of this letter is being sent to the Recording Secretary.
> Sincerely yours,
>
> George White
> Member, Second District

A member who has tendered his resignation to take effect at a future date is entitled to exercise all rights of membership prior to that time. (6 CP Sec. 228.) His name remains on the roll until the organization is officially notified of his resignation or until it takes some action with respect thereto. (2 HP Sec. 1207.) However, where a member resigns, appointing a future day for his resignation to take effect, the organization may fill the vacancy before that date. (2 HP Sec. 1229.) Indeed, an organization may always act with respect to a vacancy in a member's seat, even in the absence of a signed resignation, on the basis of factual information that the member has in fact resigned. (2 HP Sec. 1197.)

Once a member has resigned, the organization may deny him permission to withdraw his resignation. (2 HP Sec. 1213.)

—11—

MEETINGS

Sec. 88. Kinds of Meetings

There are four principal types of meetings that are available to membership organizations for the transaction of business. They are (1) regular meetings, (2) special meetings, (3) called meetings, and (4) adjourned meetings.

A *regular meeting* is one that is held at the time and place specified for the organization by its constitution or by some other directive having the force of law. A *special meeting* is one called for a special purpose or purposes or one limited to particular business. A *called meeting* is one that is held at a time other than that specified by the constitution or bylaws, but that has been assembled pursuant to an authorized call or notice.

An *adjourned meeting* is a continuation of a prior regular or special meeting that was terminated by a notice to adjourn or recess to a later time. The second meeting at the later time is thus an adjourned meeting of the first. Holding an adjourned meeting is often preferable to holding another special or called meeting because no special notice, other than that provided by the motion, need be given. An adjourned meeting is legally a continuation of the previous meeting, and those assembled can do any act that might have been done if no adjournment had taken place.[1]

All official business of a membership organization must be transacted at a legally authorized meeting. Business conducted at an unauthorized time may be invalidated.[2]

Sec. 89. Time and Place

The bylaws of a membership organization should provide for regularly scheduled periodic sessions or conventions. These are usually held annually or biannually, but may be semiannual, monthly, or

[1]*Black's Law Dictionary*, 4th ed.

[2]Sutherland, *Statutes and Statutory Construction*, 3rd ed. (1943), Sec. 401.

other specified time. Thus, the bylaws might provide that the organization "shall meet for ten days beginning on the first Monday in August of each year." The frequency of meetings within the session or convention will depend on the extent of business that must ordinarily be disposed of by the membership.

Time of Meeting

Although the constitution or bylaws of a membership organization should provide for the time of meeting, such directives should be sufficiently flexible to permit the membership to alter such time when the necessity arises. The bylaws may declare, for example, that the membership is to assemble on a specified date at least once in every year, unless it appoints a different day. (Based on the 20th Amendment, U.S. Constitution.) Under such a provision, where the organization wishes to hold a meeting at some time other than that specified in its bylaws or constitution, it may do so by a resolution duly adopted and agreed to by the membership. The organization may, pursuant to the resolution, set a different time, either earlier or later than that specified. (1 Hinds' Precedents[3] Secs. 3-6.) Such a meeting may be provided for by the organization at the time of an adjournment. (1 HP Sec. 5.)

There is some authority to the effect that where an organization meets on a day earlier than that specified in its constitution or bylaws, it may remain in continuous session to a time beyond that so specified. (1 HP Sec. 6.) However, a special or called meeting terminates by operation of law when the moment of time arrives for the organization to convene for its regular annual session under its constitution. (2 HP Sec. 1160.) Indeed, the modern view is that *any* pending session ends with the day appointed by the constitution for the regular annual session or meeting. (See House Rules Sec. 45.)

The bylaws should not set forth the daily hour of *every* meeting, because most organizations need flexibility in this regard. When meetings customarily extend over a period of several days, the bylaws should set the hour of assembly for the first day only, leaving the membership free to adopt a resolution fixing the daily hour of meeting on subsequent days. (See House Rules Sec. 6.) Such resolutions expire with the session. (1 HP Secs. 104-9.) By a custom having the force of common law, when the hour for the beginning of a regular meeting is not specified in the constitution

[3]Hereinafter cited as HP.

or bylaws, or by resolution, the organization meets at 12:00 noon. (1 HP Sec. 210.)

As noted above, the bylaws should set the time for the daily hour for the beginning of the first meeting in a session or convention, whereas the daily hour for the convening of the remaining meetings in the session should be set by resolution. This resolution, which may be agreed to even prior to the election of a chairman, may read as follows:

> *Resolved*, That the daily sessions of [NAME OF ORGANIZATION] during its 1974 Annual Meeting shall begin at [TIME OF DAY]. [1 HP Sec. 104.]

Or,

> *Resolved*, That the daily hour of meeting be fixed at [TIME OF DAY] until otherwise ordered. [1 HP Sec. 105.]

The distinction as to whether the daily hour of meeting is set by bylaw or by resolution is an important one; for if the daily hour of meeting is set by bylaw or by standing rule, a change in such time may require a motion to suspend the rules, and thereby involve notice to the membership, a two-thirds vote, etc. On the other hand, if the daily hour of meeting is set by simple resolution, it may be changed from time to time by simple resolution. (1 HP Secs. 113, 116.)

Place of Meeting

The exact location of the annual or other regular meeting should not be spelled out in detail in an organization's constitution or bylaws. Most membership organizations need flexibility in this regard so as to be able to change the place of the annual meeting from year to year, and should not have to amend the constitution or bylaws to do so. The board of directors, for example, will often wish to change the geographic location of the annual meeting from city to city, depending upon the current needs of the membership, the facilities available at a particular location, and the like.

Sec. 90. Notice of Meetings

The *regular* meetings of an organization—that is, meetings of which the time and place are set forth in the constitution or bylaws—need not be preceded by any special notice to the membership. However, for reasons noted above, it is customary to give such notice, spelling out exact details as to both time and place.

On the other hand, as a matter of law, full and timely notice must also be given of any *special* meeting or session. The proceedings of a meeting are illegal and void if it appears that one or more members were improperly notified[4] or where the notice itself was not in proper form.

The notice given to the membership of a special meeting is invalid if it does not clearly indicate each item of business to be taken up at the meeting.[5] In other words, the nature of the business that can be transacted at a special meeting is limited by the scope of the notice given thereof; matters not identified in the notice cannot legally be considered.[6]

Most membership organizations supplement the official notice with various informal notices, such as announcements used as stuffers in outgoing mail, postcards, and the like. And newspapers are alerted to the meeting by publicity releases that give the names of special speakers, as well as the date, place, and time.

The bylaws of a membership organization should provide that notice of the annual meeting is to be mailed to each member at his last-known address at least twenty days in advance of the meeting. The notice may be brief and to the point, stating only the date, time, and place. However, it is permissible to include much other information in the notice, designed merely to stimulate interest in the meeting and to increase member attendance.

An example of a terse, but legally sufficient, notice of an annual meeting is set out below:

> Cleveland, Ohio
> April 1, 1974

Dear Member:

The annual meeting of the Ohio Dentists' Association will commence at 9:00 a.m. on April 23, 1974, at the Cleveland Municipal Auditorium, and conclude on April 27, 1974. You are urged to attend.

> Sincerely yours,
>
> Charles Smith
> Chief Executive

The same notice, drafted to stimulate interest and increase

---

[4]*Haines* v. *Readfield* 41 Me. 246.

[5]*Coon Valley* v. *Spellum* 190 Wis. 140, 208 N.W. 916; *Tandy and Fairleigh Tobacco Co.* v. *Hopkinsville* 174 Ky. 189, 192 S.W. 46.

[6]See *Gray* v. *Christian Society* 137 Mass. 329.

member turnout, but still satisfying all legal requirements, might read as follows:

April 23, 1974!
Circle this date on your calendar!

That's the date for the start of the annual meeting of the Ohio Dentists' Association. We know that you'll want to attend! The meeting will be held in the Cleveland Municipal Auditorium and will start promptly at 9:00 a.m.

An exceptionally fine program has been arranged. There will be interesting reports, as well as plenty of entertainment.

A copy of the agenda for the program is enclosed. You will note that Dean Rogers from the State Dental College will be with us again. The Dean's talks are always interesting.

The Auditor's report, which will be streamlined and modernized through the use of understandable charts, will convey good news to the members. We have just completed one of our most successful seasons, and we are anxious to tell you about it.

There will be adequate time to discuss our common problems, as well as to renew old friendships. Come prepared to take part. The meeting will wind up on April 27.

Charles Smith
Chief Executive

P.S. Don't forget the date, April 23. We'll be looking forward to seeing you.

Sec. 91. Annual Meetings

The official purpose of the annual meeting is to review the business of the organization for the past year, hold elections, and plan future activities. For most membership organizations, the annual meeting is the high-water mark of the year. Usually lasting from five to ten days, the annual meeting is a time when management gives an accounting to the members, and when the members express their views to the board of directors and the staff.

The annual meeting is a requirement imposed by the bylaws, and sometimes by state statute. Legal matters that must be disposed of include nominating and electing directors, receiving official reports, and voting on bylaw changes.

In organizing the annual meeting, the organization's chief officer should appoint a number of special committees to work with the organization's officers and directors. Among those committees that should be appointed are a program committee, a resolutions committee, and various nominating committees. A chairman should be appointed for each committee. In larger organizations local committees may be appointed at the district level to contribute suggestions, contact the members, and otherwise assist in the arrangements for the annual meeting.

Sec. 92. Planning and Scheduling

Advance planning is essential to any well-organized annual meeting. The responsibility for this planning rests on the board of directors and the chief executive. Their planning must include arranging for the time and place of the meeting (unless otherwise specified by the bylaws) and organizing the program.

The key to any successful annual meeting lies in the quality of the planning that goes into it. The arrangements for a meeting hall, for example, must be made at least two months in advance of the meeting. In fact, some large organizations set the date and arrange for a meeting hall as much as three or four years in advance. Similarly, invitations to, and acceptances by, principal speakers who are to address the membership should be accomplished well in advance of the meeting. In summary, there are literally hundreds of details that must be planned and executed according to a prearranged schedule. Set out below is a checklist of some of the more important steps that should be taken in advance of the meeting to ensure its success.

ANNUAL MEETING PLAN CHECKLIST

1.   Hold annual meeting planning conference and appoint special committees with responsibilities for planning various aspects of the meeting.

2.   Appoint committees for such major jobs as the analysis and screening of resolutions and the preparation of election nominations.

3.   Settle on a date, time, and place of the meeting that is consistent with the bylaws.

4.   Reserve a meeting hall if this has not already been done.

5.   Plan a conference with auditors on the scope and presentation of the annual audit.

6.   Establish a budget for the meeting.

7.   Prepare summaries of each annual report to be presented to the membership and circulate to key officers.

8.   Prepare annual meeting notice for mailing to members as required by bylaws.

9.   Mail annual meeting notice in accordance with bylaws.

10.   Alert the secretary that minutes of the last annual meeting may need to be read or summarized and that a roll of the membership should be prepared for a roll call.

11.   Consider whether reminder notices should be sent to all members.

12.   Contact committee chairmen as to the readiness of committee reports.

13.   Prepare summary of old business to be taken up.

14.   Prepare summary of new business to be taken up.

15.   Prepare meeting agenda.

16.   Prepare printed ballots, if necessary or required.

17.   Prepare facilities for the registration of members.

Although he is usually not required to do so by the bylaws, the presiding officer together with the recording secretary should, at the conclusion of the annual meeting, prepare a summary of its most significant accomplishments. Such a summary is helpful both to members who attended and to those who were absent. Since many organizations do well to achieve a 40 percent turnout of members at an annual meeting, follow-up reports and summaries of this nature are especially important.

Sec. 93. Informal or "Committee of the Whole" Meetings

Legislative bodies have a parliamentary procedure by which the membership can resolve itself into a "committee of the whole." This is done so that the membership can consider a subject under the informal procedures of committees. In the U.S. House of Representatives, for example, the membership may resolve itself into a committee of the whole, which is presided over by a chairman who is appointed by the Speaker. Certain types of bills, such as revenue bills, have precedence before the committee. Other business may be taken up in such order as the committee may decide, unless the bill to be considered was determined by the House at the time of going into committee. (See Rule XXIII, House Rules.)

Some membership organizations have found that informal committee of the whole meetings provide a desirable forum for expediting organization business. Others use a procedure for informal consideration pursuant to motion. For example, a member may rise and state: "It is common knowledge among members that we have outgrown the building we now occupy. I move that we consider on an informal basis the problem of purchasing or leasing new facilities for this organization."

Under either system, the person selected to preside and to guide the discussion serves, in effect, as chairman of these informal meetings. The subject is presented, discussed, and voted upon in much the same way as it would be if taken up by a committee.

The primary advantages of the committee of the whole meeting are the smaller quorum requirements, the expeditious five-minute rule for debate, and the reading of resolutions by paragraph or section, rather than in its entirety.

The business affairs of an organization are commonly taken up in committee of the whole or informal meetings. In such cases, a member of the organization's staff, such as a department head, may be selected to act as a chairman so as to present the problem to the membership in the clearest possible terms. This gives the membership a chance to get the business information in question from the person who is directly responsible therefor. And it has the added advantage of giving the members a better chance of getting acquainted with key employees.

Sec. 94. Limiting Attendance; Secret Meetings

Some organizations may wish to have meetings that are closed to the public or subject to other attendance limitations. If so, the bylaws or standing rules should specify those persons who are to be permitted to attend the meetings of the organization, as shown below.

> The persons hereinafter named, and none other, shall be admitted to the meeting of [NAME OF ORGANIZATION]: qualified members in good standing; elected or appointed officers; consultants to committees when business from their committee is under consideration. It shall not be in order for the Presiding Officer to entertain a request for the suspension of this rule, even by unanimous consent. [Based on Rule XXXII, House Rules Sec. 919.]

During its initial organizational meeting and prior to the adoption of the rules, the membership may agree to a special order regulating the admission of persons to the meetings. For example, the members may agree that it shall be:

> *Ordered*, That the Doorkeeper be directed to enforce those rules of the prior session [*or convention*] as relate to the admission of persons to meetings. [1 HP Sec. 96.]

A membership organization may also provide in its bylaws for secret sessions. For example, the bylaws may state:

> Whenever confidential communications are received, or whenever the Presiding Officer informs the membership that he has communications that he believes ought to be kept secret for the present, the meeting shall be cleared of all persons except the members and officers of the organization, until otherwise ordered by a vote of the membership. [See Rule XXIX, House Rules.]

Any motion to remove the injunction of secrecy must also be made behind closed doors. (5 HP Sec. 7254.) The reason behind this rule is that open debate on the motion could well lead to open discussion of the confidential material or subject.

Sec. 95. Effect of Recess or Adjournment

A question sometimes arises as to the handling of business that remains undisposed of at the end of a convention. It is a settled rule, dating from the time of Jefferson's Manual, that matters pending at the time of termination of a convention are, upon adjournment, discontinued, and, if taken up subsequently, must be taken up *de novo*. (See House Rules Sec. 588.)

However, in the interest of efficiency and expediency, the bylaws should provide for the continuation of business from meeting to meeting within the same session or convention as if no adjournment had taken place. Thus, the bylaws should contain language to the effect that:

> All business before [NAME OF ORGANIZATION] at the end of one meeting shall be resumed at the commencement of the next meeting of the same session in the same manner as if no adjournment had taken place. [See Rule XXVI, House Rules Sec. 901.]

Of course, irrespective of the bylaws, it is recognized that recesses taken during a session or convention, pursuant to a motion to recess, are no more than continuances from one day to another or for some other brief period, and that all matters pending at these times remain in status quo; under this view, when the membership reassembles after a recess, matters pending at the conclusion of the prior meeting are resumed regardless of the order of business at the point at which they were left. (See House Rules Sec. 588.)

—12—

CONDUCTING BUSINESS AT MEETINGS

Sec. 96. The Presiding Officer

The presence of a presiding officer is indispensable to the conducting of regular business of an organization. In the absence of the presiding officer an organization must adjourn unless some other person has been authorized to preside over the busines of the organization. The clerk (or secretary) ceases to preside with the election of a presiding officer, so it is not competent for him to act upon any business other than a motion to elect a presiding officer or a motion to adjourn. (1 Hinds' Precedents[1] Secs. 227, 228.) In the event of the death of the presiding officer, the clerk at its next meeting calls the assembly to order, ascertains the presence of a quorum, and presides over the proceedings to elect a successor. (House Rules Sec. 28.)

There is no doubt that the presiding officer is the key to any successful meeting. He is, at one and the same time, captain of the team, timekeeper, and master of ceremonies. Everything is in his hands, from the time he calls the meeting to order until the time he announces it adjourned. He has the responsibility for keeping the meeting running smoothly and headed in the right direction. He must know how to get the meeting started and, equally important, how and when to stop.

The primary functions of the presiding officer are to (1) ensure that business is brought before the membership in an orderly and parliamentary fashion, (2) be strictly impartial, unbiased, and fair

[1]Hereinafter cited as HP.

to all members, (3) keep the meeting moving, and (4) preserve order.

A successful presiding officer must follow "Caesar's wife" concepts from the very outset of the meeting. He not only must be fair but must, in addition, *appear* to be fair. He must by his attitude indicate a desire to be fair and impartial to all members. He should put aside his personal views on any given issue and must give each side an equal opportunity to be heard.

Although the presiding officer should put his personal preferences aside, in most membership organizations he is permitted to relinquish the chair to the vice-president or vice-chairman and to express his views from the floor, just as any other member. In such instances, however, he must not return to the chair until the particular matter is settled or voted upon. He should bear in mind, furthermore, that he may lose his appearance of impartiality should he take sides too frequently in debate.

The presiding officer must see to it that the meeting is conducted in an orderly and businesslike manner. He should not permit a member to have the floor without first addressing the chair, nor should he permit members to talk back and forth in such a way as to disrupt the meeting. He may remind the members from time to time that before a matter can be discussed officially, a motion must first be made and that discussion may then follow.

The presiding officer at a meeting must have a comprehensive knowledge of all the business of the organization, especially that which is to come before the membership at the meeting. He must also be tactful, courteous, and at the same time businesslike and firm. Above all, he should have a good grasp of parliamentary procedure. He must know the parliamentary tools that will enable him to keep the discussion or debate focused on the problem at hand. A thorough understanding of parliamentary law will enable him to guide the meeting and yet not coerce the members.

Although the presiding officer of a membership organization normally has a number of assistants, he has many duties that cannot be delegated. He must call the meeting to order, dispose of the organization's business in the sequence in which it is scheduled, and proceed on a step-by-step basis. He should recognize members who wish to speak when they have a right to do so under the standing rules of the organization.

From time to time he will find it necessary to restate motions to make certain that all members have heard them. If the motion is a procedural motion, he should, if called upon by way of a parliamentary inquiry, explain the manner in which the procedural motion relates to the main motion.

Sec. 97. Calling the Roll

Calling the roll of members may be made a mandatory step under the bylaws. Even where not required by the bylaws, the calling of the roll is one means of establishing the presence of a quorum. (Quorum requirements, see Secs. 102 *et seq. infra.*)

Of course, in large organizations, with perhaps thousands of members in attendance, it is impractical to read aloud the entire roll of members. In such organizations it is sometimes permissible under the bylaws for a credentials committee to prepare a list of registered members in attendance and to report thereon to the membership. The membership may then, pursuant to motion, adopt this list as the official roll of voting members. This list should be revised and updated by the credentials committee from time to time so that it can be referred to when a question arises as to the presence of a quorum or for some other reason.

It is desirable that the roll always be called in some established and orderly sequence, so that each member can anticipate when his name is likely to be called. The roll may be called in alphabetical order by name, although in many organizations the call of the roll is in alphabetical order of names of members grouped or classified by state, county, district, or other region. (1 HP Sec. 64.) In the U.S. House of Representatives, when the House is first organized and the clerk discharges the duty of calling the House to order, he calls the roll of members by states. Thereafter, the roll is called alphabetically by the members' names, irrespective of state names. (1 HP Sec. 83.)

The initial roll call should include the names of all persons who are members in good standing and whose credentials are in proper order. The fact that someone has lost his credentials does not justify adding his name to the roll at this time. If, after the organization of the membership, it clearly appears that his qualifications are in no way disputed, he may be seated. (1 HP Sec. 85.)

The clerk should refuse to permit the interruption of this roll call, especially by one not on the roll. (1 HP Sec. 84.) When the roll call has been completed, with members present responding, the clerk may present a tabulated statement of the changes in membership that have occurred since the last regular session or meeting. (1 HP Sec. 81.)

Sec. 98. Order of Business

In most membership organizations, particular kinds of business are taken up in an established sequence. This sequence is called the order of business and is generally fixed by the bylaws. An established order of business is most important because it enables the members to know when they are likely to be called upon to participate, to vote, and what matters they may be called to vote on.

The order of business may be changed where it will enable the meeting to proceed more efficiently and expeditiously and where the membership can be advised in advance of the change. However, the order of business can only be changed by motion to suspend the rules or, in some organizations, by unanimous consent.

The order of business at the annual meeting for membership organizations generally includes reading and approval of the minutes, hearing annual reports of officers and committees, electing directors and other officers, disposing of unfinished business, taking up new business, and adjournment.

At the first meeting of a session, if a quorum is present, the clerk announces that fact and declares that the next business in order is the election of a presiding officer. (1 HP Sec. 81.) During this initial period, even before the election of a presiding officer, the organization is technically in session, and business transacted at such time is valid and binding. (1 HP Sec. 87.) At the opening of a meeting other than the first, the presiding officer calls the organization to order. When the number of members present is ascertained, he announces the presence of a quorum (if such be the fact), and the organization is ready to proceed to the business at hand. (1 HP Sec. 81.)

The proper sequence for taking up business is set out below.

1. *Call to order.* A call to order is effectuated simply by the announcement by the presiding officer: "The meeting will please come to order."

2. *Invocation or prayer.* If an invocation or prayer is to be said, the presiding officer calls upon someone present, often a minister, priest, or rabbi.

3. *Roll call.* The presiding officer should ask the clerk or recording secretary to call the roll when necessary to ensure the presence of a quorum, or where it is mandatory under the bylaws. In organizations with large memberships, the roll of members is not

read aloud, the bylaws permitting instead a report of the credentials committee on its official roll of members.

4. *Minutes of the previous meeting.* The presiding officer may call for a reading of the minutes of the previous meeting and must do so if a proper motion to that effect is made. A reading of the minutes is sometimes a bylaw requirement but is frequently dispensed with by unanimous consent. If the minutes are read, the presiding officer should call for any corrections or additions. He then may declare the minutes approved as read or corrected, or he may entertain a motion to that effect.

5. *Reports.* Following the approval of the minutes, the presiding officer may call for committee reports.

6. *Old business.* Unfinished business should follow the presentation of committee reports. The presiding officer should declare that "unfinished business is now in order" and state the business. The secretary or other officer should be given the duty of maintaining a record of old business, which should be given to the presiding officer as required and which may include motions postponed from a previous meeting.

7. *New business.* The presiding officer announces: "New business is in order." If he knows of certain matters that have not been brought up by motion from the floor, as scheduled, he should so state, and ask members if they care to make any motion on the matters suggested.

8. *Announcements.* Members may make arrangements with the presiding officer that will permit them to make announcements from the floor. Following these announcements, the chairman makes his own announcements.

9. *Adjournment.* When a motion to adjourn is made and agreed to, the presiding officer should announce the meeting adjourned, even though other business may be pending. Sometimes he merely states, "Without objection, the meeting is adjourned." Pending business must be put over to the next meeting.

Sec. 99. Agendas

A well-organized and detailed agenda or program, patterned after the order of business as set forth in the bylaws, is essential to the success of any annual meeting. It should be circulated to all concerned well in advance. A sample program follows:

SAMPLE ANNUAL MEETING PROGRAM

PRESIDING OFFICER'S CHECKLIST
FIRST DAY

9:00 A.M.
1. Call the meeting to order.
2. Order members roll call where necessary or required to ensure quorum.
3. Instruct the clerk or secretary to read the official notice of the
   meeting and order the notice and any accompanying af-
   fidavits to be filed with the minutes of the meeting.
4. Instruct the clerk to read the minutes of the last meeting, or
   ask for unanimous consent to waive this procedure.
   a. If the minutes are read, ask if there are any corrections or
      additions. If none, state that the minutes will stand ap-
      proved as read.
5. State purpose of meeting.
   a. To elect two directors for three years to fill two expiring
      terms.
   b. To give members an opportunity to propose resolutions
      and offer motions to express their views regarding their
      organization.
6. State briefly the program for the day.
   a. Describe the main features of the morning program, to
      include a report of the board of directors.
   b. Describe the main features of the afternoon program, to
      include an annual business report, various committee re-
      ports, and the election of directors.
   c. State time of adjournment.

10:30 A.M.
1. Introduce keynote speaker.

11:00 A.M.
1. Present the board of directors' report, using a previously
   prepared outline.
   a. Ask board members for any additional comment.
   b. Call on the organization's members or their designated
      leaders for questions concerning the report.

12:00 noon.
1. Announce a recess until 1:15 P.M. and briefly review the
   afternoon program.

1:15 P.M.
1. Call the meeting to order and announce the intention that
   the meeting will adjourn promptly at 5:00 P.M.

2. Call on the executive director to present the annual business report and announce that the membership has designated certain leaders to ask questions after the presentation of this and other staff reports. Identify and introduce the designated leaders.

1:45 P.M.

1. Call for the financial report of the treasurer.

2:15 P.M.

1. Call for questions from previously identified leaders.
2. Call for additional questions from the membership at large and announce the time available for such questions.
3. Call for a motion to accept the reports as presented.
4. Order report filed with minutes of meeting.

2:45 P.M.

1. Announce that committee reports are to be heard, and the amount of time available for this purpose.
2. Call on Mr. White to report for the committee that was appointed to study the advisability of purchasing a new building for the organization.
   a. Inquire as to whether there are any motions the members wish to offer on this report.
3. Call on Mr. Brown to report for the committee on group insurance.
   a. Inquire as to whether there are any motions the members wish to propose on this report.

3:00 P.M.

1. State whether there is any old or unfinished business to come before the meeting and entertain motions relative thereto.

3:30 P.M.

1. State that the organization is now ready to elect two directors for a three-year term, and explain the importance of the election.
   a. Identify the two directors whose terms expire.
   b. Identify the members of the nominating committee and indicate how their nominations were made.
2. Call Mr. Black, chairman of the nominating committee, to make the report of that committee.
3. Call for any nominations from the floor.
   a. Permit the person making a nomination to comment briefly on the experience and qualifications of the person he has nominated.
4. State that a motion is in order for the nominations to be closed.

5. Introduce those persons nominated.
6. Announce that the vote is on the election of nominees and instruct members that they are to vote for only two of the candidates nominated.
7. Order the collection and counting of the ballots.
8. Announce the results of the election; express the appreciation of the association to the retiring directors.

4:15 P.M.

1. Announce that new business before the meeting is now in order.
   a. Announce the time to be allowed for each motion and discussion thereon.
   b. After each vote announce whether the motion has carried or failed.

5:00 P.M.

1. Call for motion to adjourn.

Sec. 100. Committee and Staff Reports

Committee reports should be used to bring the membership up to date on the affairs of the organization and the conditions under which it operates. Time should be scheduled following each report for the hearing of resolutions and discussion concerning them.

Committee reports should be prepared and distributed well in advance of the meeting at which they are to be presented. This is most useful to the officers of the organization, for it will enable them to anticipate to some extent those questions that are likely to come before the membership before they vote. Advance distribution of committee reports also enables the membership to vote more intelligently and with less digression at the meeting.

A successful meeting often depends in a large measure on how well the various committeemen and committee chairmen carry their assigned tasks. Above all, they should be fully prepared and ready with their report when it is to be presented at a meeting to the membership. It is the responsibility of each chairman to see to it that his committee's work is finished on schedule. On the date that his committee is to report, he should be ready at all times to receive a call from the presiding officer to present his report. When the meeting is over, each chairman of each committee should see that the information gathered by his committee is preserved and passed on so as to be available to similar committees in future years.

At the annual meeting it is customary to hear various staff reports on the affairs of the association for the preceding twelve months. It should be determined in advance whether these reports are to be summarized or read in full, and whether they might be supplemented with various graphic illustrations. The treasurer's report, for example, may consist of a simple operating statement and a balance sheet, coupled with some financial graphs for easy analysis and understanding.

Financial statements, whether in detail or in summary form, should be presented by a qualified officer who is sufficiently well prepared to answer questions at the conclusion of his report. A statement of income and expense, current balance sheet, or data showing assets, liabilities, net worth, and operating costs should be fully explained and may be compared with those of previous years. Technical language, such as "reserves" or "net income," should be explained.

In this connection it may be desirable to distribute copies of the operating statement or balance sheet to the membership or its designated leaders, so that specific items in the financial report can be discussed following its presentation.

Following the presentation of committee reports, it is customary to hear various resolutions as suggested by those reports. The voting on these resolutions should be handled in an orderly and parliamentary manner, according to a carefully planned timetable or a schedule. A fixed time should be allotted to each proposed resolution. Resolutions should not be permitted unless they have been reviewed by a resolutions committee and the parliamentarian.

Sec. 101. Minutes of Meetings; Journals

A membership organization should maintain a journal, minutes, or other official record of each day's proceedings. At the beginning of each daily meeting, it is customary in many organizations for the clerk or secretary to read, in summary form, the record of the previous day's meeting, and for the membership to approve such record. (4 HP Secs. 2730 *et seq.*) The purpose of reading the minutes of the previous meeting is to permit corrections to be made, to provide continuity, and to give the members a point of departure in taking up old business and in moving on to new business. The minutes should provide an accurate record of the proceedings and are especially important when the organization becomes involved in some legal action concerning its activities.

The minutes or other official record of the business of the organization should be prepared and read notwithstanding the incapacity of the clerk or other official responsible for it. (1 HP Sec. 237.) However, to save time, some organizations have a procedure by which the reading and correction of the minutes is referred to a minutes committee. Moreover, in the event that the press of business on any particular day is so great as to prevent the reading and approval of the proceedings of a previous day or days, the journals for a series of days may be read and approved at one time. (1 HP Sec. 92.)

The minutes of the meetings of an organization are open to inspection by any member who wishes to see them. During the meeting, the clerk should take extensive notes and then prepare a formal draft after the meeting is concluded. The minutes should be kept in a special book that contains the minutes of other meetings.

The minutes should contain a record of all official business, including motions or resolutions proposed, committee reports as submitted, voting results, elections, and the like. The minutes should disclose the type of meeting—that is, whether regular or special—the place, date, and time, and the name of the presiding officer. The minutes should include notations as to all formal actions taken, but need not incorporate the text of speeches or other oratory.

The outcome of all votes should be reflected in the minutes. If the votes are counted, as in the case of a roll call vote, the number of votes for and the number of votes against should be specified in the minutes. (Cf. 1 HP Sec. 232.)

All committee reports that are submitted at a meeting should be identified in the minutes. If copies of these reports are not routinely distributed to all members, the minutes should indicate where these reports are maintained or filed.

The clerk or recording secretary should begin reading the minutes of the previous meeting when he is instructed to do so by the presiding officer. When this has been done, the presiding officer may say, "Are there any corrections to the minutes?" If there is no response, he then says, "If not, they stand approved as read."

If a member offers corrections to the minutes, the presiding officer should call for the approval of the membership. He does this either by calling for the adoption of the corrections by unanimous consent or, if there is a dissent, by putting the suggested corrections to a vote. When this has been done, the presiding officer may then say, "If there are no further corrections, the minutes will stand approved as corrected." When the membership has signified its approval of the minutes, either with or without corrections, the clerk writes the word "approved" at the bottom of the minutes, notes the date and time, and adds his signature.

It should be borne in mind that the minutes of a meeting may be of critical importance in the event that the organization should become involved in any antitrust litigation. Since minutes are a reasonably contemporaneous report of what happened at a meeting, the courts tend to give them credence as to what occurred. For this reason, all minutes of meetings, including the minutes of the board of directors, should be carefully reviewed by the organization's legal counsel as well as its officers.

The minutes may also be relevant in determining various tax questions. For example, to establish the deductibility of the cost of travel for the wife of an officer of a membership organization, the minutes of a meeting might show a resolution providing for the payment of travel expenses of the wife in connection with some official function given to her to perform at the meeting.

Sec. 102. Establishing a Quorum

In the House, as in all membership organizations, a quorum is necessary to the transaction of business.[2] A quorum is the number of members required by law or by the bylaws to be present at a member meeting where official business is to be carried on. In Congress, under the Constitution, a majority of each House constitutes a quorum.

Sometimes a quorum is expressed as a percentage of the membership. If so, a quorum is that percentage of total members in good standing who must be present at the meeting in order for it legally to transact business. If a quorum is not present, the presiding officer may not entertain business except for the purpose of voting to adjourn. (6 Cannon's Precedents[3] Sec. 680.) A quorum is not required on a vote to adjourn. (4 HP Sec. 2998.)

It is advisable to keep the quorum relatively small if this is permissible under state law. If the quorum is set too high, it may at

[2]See U.S. Constitution, Art. I, Sec. 5.

[3]Hereinafter cited as CP.

times present difficulties in getting enough members together at a meeting to transact business.

Many membership organizations require different quorums for different kinds of business; thus, it is most important that the bylaws define the requirements of a quorum. In the absence of a specific definition, it is the general rule that 50 percent of the members, plus one, of an organization constitute a quorum.

Where the constitution or bylaws state that a majority shall constitute a quorum to do business, a question arises as to whether this means a majority of the total possible membership or merely a majority of those members duly seated and qualified during any particular term. On the one hand, it can be argued that a failure to seat a majority of the total possible representation would bring the organization to a complete stop. In opposition to this view, it might be argued that a small fraction of the whole might gain control of the organization. In the U.S. House of Representatives a quorum is a majority of the members actually sworn in and entitled to seats at the time, and not a majority of the total possible membership. (1 HP Sec. 630; 4 HP Secs. 2889, 2890; 6 CP Sec. 638.)

—13—

COMMITTEES

Sec. 103. Kinds of Committees

One of the outstanding characteristics of membership organizations the world over is the powerful role played by committees in setting policy and in carrying out their objectives. The Congress, state legislatures, business associations, and countless clubs and societies have traditionally conducted their work through committees of their members.

There are four principal types of committees (Rule XI, House Rules):

1. Standing or permanent committees that continue from year to year.
2. Special, select, or temporary committees created for a particular purpose or time frame.
3. Joint committees.
4. Subcommittees, both standing and select.

Committees may also be classified by function, such as:

1. Committees with original jurisdiction, as defined in the organization's rules, over one or more subjects of special interest to the general membership.
2. Supervisory committees, which are concerned with the operation or administration of the organization.
3. Fiscal committees, which are concerned with financial affairs of various kinds.
4. Investigating committees, which may be established on a permanent or select basis to make inquiries under the direction of the general membership.
5. Housekeeping committees, which oversee the internal affairs of an organization.
6. Policy or political committees, which perform functions relating to political matters or public affairs.

Every membership organization should define the jurisdiction of its standing committees in the organization's rules. The interests of the organization should be divided into distinct categories, as defined in the rules. Then, as resolutions or other matters are introduced, they may be referred to the appropriate standing committee, which will then consider and report on them so that they can be taken up on the floor. (Rule XI, House Rules.) The trend is for the standing committee to make recommendations that the organization's membership usually find useful and educational.

Two committees common to most legislative membership organizations are a rules committee, discussed below, and a committee on committees. It is the practice of many such organizations for a committee on committees to prepare lists of committee assignments, these lists being drawn up by the major parties in party conference and then ratified by the general membership.

Most nonlegislative membership organizations have an executive committee to carry out policies adopted by the board or by the membership as a whole. These committees generally consist of three to five members. Other common types of committees include:

1. *Resolutions committee.* Reviews the language of all proposed resolutions and schedules their presentation to the membership.
2. *Bylaw committee.* Prepares drafts of bylaws for presentation to the board of directors and the general membership.
3. *Program committee.* Helps to plan and carry out meetings of the membership, especially annual meetings.
4. *Nominating committee.* Identifies individuals willing and qualified to serve as an official or a presiding officer.
5. *Tellers committee.* Distributes and counts votes and ballots.

In most membership organizations, the committes report to the board of directors or other governing body. However, in some institutions the committees report to the president of the organization, to the chief staff executive, to the general membership, or to a section or division of the organization.

Sec. 104. Committee Chairmen and Members

Although there are a few nonlegislative membership organizations that elect the chairmen of their committees, in the great majority of such organizations committee chairmen are appointed by the president or other chief elected officer.

In the House, until 1911, the Speaker generally appointed the chairmen and the members of the standing and select committees. In that year, however, this power was taken from the Speaker, and since that time the committees and their chairmen have been elected by the House. (4 Hinds' Precedents[1] Sec. 4513; 8 Cannon's Precedents[2] Sec. 2201-2.)

In filling vacancies in committee chairmanships, the unwritten rule of seniority has usually, but not invariably, been followed. Seniority is the custom by which the chairmanships of the standing committees go to the members who have the longest continuous service on the committees.

Similar criteria have been used in making committee assignments among members. The most common considerations are seniority of service, geography, personal preference, and previous committee service. Seniority is governed by continuous, uninterrupted service; a member's seniority dates from the beginning of his last uninterrupted service, regardless of previous service, and determines his rank on committees.

A few membership organizations periodically poll the membership to determine individual preference for committee service.

It is not necessary that the bylaws establish a limit on the length of service for committee members. Indeed, most membership organizations do not have a fixed or customary maximum length of service for committee members. Where a maximum length for committee service is set, the usual period is for one year.

Sec. 105. Committee on Rules

A rules committee is doubtless the most influential committee that exists among American membership organizations. There has always been a Committee on Rules in the House of Representatives. For many years it was the practice of the House to set up a select committee at the beginning of each Congress authorized to report a system of rules. Many additional powers have been given to it from time to time. In the 1840s it was held that the committee might "report from time to time," and this ruling was sustained on appeal. This was the first in a series of innovations that gave the Committee on Rules special privileges over the handling of particular bills. (5 HP Sec. 6780.)

[1] Hereinafter cited as HP.
[2] Hereinafter cited as CP.

Later the House upheld a ruling that the committee might properly report a special order providing for the consideration of a particular bill. (4 HP Sec. 3160.) This ruling initiated the modern practice whereby the Rules Committee reports special orders, resolutions, or "rules" that provide times and methods for the consideration of special bills or classes of bills. Under this procedure the House may take up particular legislation by majority vote instead of being forced to rely on suspension of the rules, which requires a two-thirds vote, or unanimous consent. The system provides an efficient means of bringing up for consideration bills difficult to reach in the regular order and for confining the consideration of bills within specified limits. (4 HP Sec. 3152.)

In 1920 it was held that the committee might "report a resolution providing for the consideration of a bill which has not yet been introduced." (8 CP Sec. 3388.) A few years later, the committee's right to report a resolution for consideration of a bill on which the House had refused to act under suspension of the rules was upheld. (8 CP Sec. 3389.) Thus, the Rules Committee can control much of the business coming from the other committees of the House, decide which bills shall be cleared for consideration on the floor, and significantly influence the order in which they shall be taken up. Through its power to report new business, it has original as well as secondary jurisdiction. The committee can also determine the procedural conditions under which the House considers most substantive measures, including the duration of debate and the extent to which a measure may be amended. It may also stipulate that all points of order against a proposition be considered as waived. Thus, the Committee on Rules is to a large degree the governing committee of the House, as it is in many membership organizations.

—14—

MOTIONS

Sec. 106. Kinds of Motions; Precedence

Motions used by membership organizations fall into four classifications, and they must be taken up and voted upon in a definite order
of preference. These classifications are (1) main motions, (2) subsidiary motions, (3) procedural motions, and (4) privileged motions.
(Motions generally, see 5 Hinds' Precedents[1] Ch. 117, and 8
Cannon's Precedents[2] Ch. 247.)

Main motions are those that formally state a question or item
of business and bring it before the membership. Main motions are
voted upon last in order of precedence. Main motions may be
divided into two basic categories: (1) those that call for some kind of
action; for example, "I move that this organization purchase a computer"; and (2) those that put the organization on record as expres-
sing some matter of policy; for example, "I move that this organization adopt the following resolution: '*Resolved*, That this organization is in favor of supporting the 1976 Bicentennial Celebration.' "

Subsidiary motions amend or in some other way alter main
motions and must therefore be considered and voted upon ahead of
the main motions to which they apply. An example of a subsidiary
motion would be, "I move to insert the words 'or lease' before the
words 'a computer.' " A motion proposing that the issues involved
in the main motion be referred to committee is also a subsidiary
motion. (See Rule XVI Clause 4, House Rules.)

Procedural motions usually involve a procedural question.
Such motions should be acted upon before either subsidiary motions or main motions in the order of precedence. For example, a
member may say, "I rise to a point of order, Mr. Chairman. The
amendment proposed is not germane to the pending resolution."
The chairman should rule on such questions before proceeding to
consideration of the pending matter. (See House Rules Sec. 627.)

[1] Hereinafter cited as HP.

[2] Hereinafter cited as CP.

Privileged motions enjoy the highest priority, and the presiding officer must put them to a vote ahead of any other pending motions. It is a general rule, dating from the time of Thomas Jefferson, that the question first moved shall be first put. But this rule gives way to what is called privileged motions and privileged questions, which are of different grades and precedence among themselves. Thus, the motion to adjourn takes precedence over all others. (See Jefferson's Manual, House Rules Secs. 437-39.) The main privileged motions, in order of their precedence, are (1) to adjourn, (2) to table, (3) for the previous question, (4) to refer, and (5) to amend. (Rule XVI Clause 4, House Rules; see also 5 HP Chs. 118-23; 8 CP Chs. 248-53.)

A motion to take up a matter of organizational or personal privilege takes precedence over all other motions except another privileged motion. For example, a member may interrupt a speaker to say, "Mr. Chairman, I rise to a point of order. The public address system is not working and we are unable to hear the speaker." At this point, it becomes the duty of the presiding officer to attend to the matter immediately, because it involves the right of a member to hear, and thus participate in, the proceedings.

Each motion before a meeting must be considered separately. When a question is being considered pursuant to a proper motion, the presiding officer may not entertain another motion unless it has a higher priority. (Priorities generally, see House Rules Sec. 782.) The priority accorded to motions is based on the relative importance of each. This ensures that questions will ultimately be resolved unless interrupted by a matter of greater weight.

In determining priorities between motions, the presiding officer should take into account the fact that certain motions, if taken up at all, must be taken up within a certain period of time. If, for example, a motion to reconsider a vote must be made at the same meeting at which the vote was taken, the presiding officer should give timely attention to such a motion. (See Rule XVIII, House Rules; motion to reconsider, see 5 HP Ch. 123 and 8 CP Ch. 253.)

Motions should be made in strict compliance with parliamentary law. A motion may be made only after the last speaker has finished his remarks, or yielded the floor; the presiding officer then recognizes the member who rises first. (House Rules Sec. 356.)

Motions that are unrelated to the business at hand should be ruled out by the presiding officer. Likewise, motions that are made solely to obstruct the transaction of business should be ruled out of order, as should dilatory motions. (Rule XVI Clause 10, House

Rules.) Whoever is acting as presiding officer enjoys these rights under parliamentary law. (Dilatory motions, see 5 HP Ch. 124 and 8 CP Ch. 254.)

Most motions are subject to debate before they are voted upon. Motions that deal with procedure are generally excepted from the operation of this rule. Since such motions are governed by parliamentary law, rather than the wishes of the members, they are not subject to debate. However, the presiding officer may recognize members to hear debate on points of order. (8 CP Secs. 3446-48.)

Motions that are debatable include main motions, motions to amend, and motions to postpone indefinitely. Debate on the motion to refer a matter to a committee is limited to issues concerning the committee itself, such as its powers and jurisdiction, and may not involve the merits of the main motion. (5 HP Secs. 5564-68; 8 CP Sec. 2740.)

A motion to rescind is used to vacate or otherwise nullify some action previously taken or to set aside a motion previously agreed to. It is not privileged. (4 HP Sec. 3383.)

Sec. 107. Stating Motions; Seconding Motions

When a member wishes to present a motion, he rises and addresses the presiding officer, using his official title or saying, "Mr. President." When he is recognized by the presiding officer, he says simply, "I move that," and makes his motion.

When a major motion has been made, it is a good practice for the presiding officer or the secretary to restate the motion to ensure that everyone has heard it and understands it. The motion may be restated by saying, "It has been moved that. . . . Does any member desire to be heard on the motion?" (See Rule I Clause 5 and Rule XVI Clause 2, House Rules.)

In the interest of accuracy and for other good reasons, all propositions and major motions should be reduced to writing. Copies thereof should be distributed in advance to key individuals, including the presiding officer and recording secretary.

Parliamentary law requires that motions be stated in their simplest form. If one motion can be made that will accomplish the same purpose as two or more consecutive motions, the one motion should be used. Thus, where the moving party wishes (1) to delete language and (2) replace it with other language, he should do so with one motion—the motion to strike and insert. (Rule XVI Clause 7, House Rules; 5 HP Sec. 6124.)

In Jefferson's time it was the rule that when a motion was made, it was not to be put to the question or debated until it was seconded. (Jefferson's Manual, House Rules, Sec. 392.) Today, however, most formal proposals receive advance study and support in committee before ever reaching the floor; therefore, with certain exceptions, such as the motion to suspend the rules, a second is not required as a prerequisite to floor consideration.

However, many membership organizations follow the general rule that when a motion is made by one member it must be seconded by another, who need not wait for recognition from the presiding officer. The theory underlying this rule is that a motion should be of interest to at least two members of an organization before it should be allowed to take up the time of the general membership.

A member who wishes to second the motion may do so by rising and addressing the chair, "I second the motion." When a motion is made that requires a second and no second is forthcoming, the presiding officer may himself call for a second to the motion, saying, "Is there a second to the motion?" If a second is still not forthcoming, he should state: "The motion may not be considered for lack of a second."

Sec. 108. Motions to Discharge

The primary purpose of a motion to discharge is to take from a committee a proposal that is opposed by a majority of the committee members or held up by the committee chairman. This motion provides a mechanism whereby a single member or group of members can present a motion to discharge any committee from further consideration of a resolution or other proposal. (See Rule XXVII Clause 4, House Rules.) Ordinarily the motion is not privileged. (4 HP Sec. 4693.)

When a discharge motion is called up, the resolution or other matter should be read to the members by title only, so as to curtail dilatory tactics of the minority. Debate on a discharge motion should be limited to ten minutes for and ten minutes against.

The discharge motion is in limited use among membership organizations generally. Many regard the frequent use of the discharge motion as an abuse of the normal legislative process. Others may be opposed to the motion simply because they want the proposal to die in committee. Still others may be considering their own possible desire to bottle up a bill in the future, and may be reluctant to use a procedure that they feel may provide the suggestion for similar action by their colleagues.

Sec. 109. Motions to Refer or Recommit

A motion to refer is a procedure used to refer a proposition to a committee for study, whereas a motion to recommit is a parliamentary device designed to return a proposal to the committee that reported it. It was Jefferson's view that after a matter had been committed and reported, "it ought not, in any ordinary course, to be recommitted." But he recognized that "in cases of importance, and for special reasons, it is sometimes recommitted, and usually to the same committee." (Jefferson's Manual, House Rules Sec. 420.)

If a motion to recommit "without instructions" (commonly called a "straight" motion) is approved, all debate ceases, and the matter is removed from consideration and returned to the committee where it originated. If a motion to recommit "with instructions" is approved, the committee must report back pursuant to those instructions. (See Rule XVI Clause 4, House Rules; 8 CP Secs. 2714, 2758, 2762.)

The motion to recommit is in order only at the conclusion of all debate. At such time the member managing debate on the resolution will move the previous question, or the previous question will be ordered by the presiding officer "without objection." After the previous question is ordered, it is in order to offer one motion to recommit, with or without instructions. (See Rule XVI Clause 4, House Rules.)

Sec. 110. Motions to Table

In Jefferson's time, when the House membership had something else that claimed its present attention, and wished to reserve its power to take up the pending matter at a later time, it would order it to lie on the table. (See Jefferson's Manual, House Rules, Sec. 445.) In other words, the motion to lay on the table (generally see 5 HP Ch. 119 and 8 CP Ch. 249) was originally used in the House merely to put a proposition aside temporarily, to be called up again whenever it suited the membership. However, the motion is now used for a final adverse disposition of the matter without debate. (5 HP Secs. 5389, 5391-95; 8 CP Secs. 2652, 2659, 3453.) It is in order before the member entitled to prior recognition for debate has begun his remarks. (5 HP Secs. 5391-95.) It is not applicable to any matter that is not debatable.

The motion to lay on the table is applicable to any debatable matter, including various other motions. However, the motion to lay on the table may not be made after the previous question is ordered. (8 CP Sec. 2655.)

When a resolution pertaining to the right of a member to a seat is proposed, the membership may either refer the matter to committee for immediate consideration or vote to table the resolution. A motion to table in such a case takes precedence over the motion to refer to committee. (6 CP Sec. 86.)

Sec. 111. Moving the Previous Question

The motion for ordering the previous question is a parliamentary device that is used to terminate further debate and amendments. (Generally, see 5 HP Ch. 120 and 8 CP Ch. 250.) It is used to end debate on the issue before the membership and requires an immediate vote without further discussion or amendment. A motion to table the motion for the previous question is not in order, and no debate is permitted on the motion itself; it must be immediately voted up or down. If the membership approves the motion, it then proceeds immediately to vote on the matter pending before it. If it votes down the motion, debate continues, control of time passes to opponents, and amendments may be in order. (See Rule XVII Clause 1, House Rules.)

It has been the rule since Jefferson's time that the motion for the previous question itself cannot be amended. Under parliamentary usage, the issue is whether the main question be now put, that is, as Jefferson reminded us, "at this instant; and as the present instant is but one, it can admit of no modification. To change it to tomorrow, or any other moment, is without example and without utility." (Jefferson's Manual, House Rules, Sec. 452.)

In the U.S. House of Representatives, if the previous question has been ordered on a proposition on which there has been no debate, any member may demand that forty minutes of debate be provided. Such time is divided equally between those in favor of the proposition and those opposed. (See House Rules Sec. 805; 5 HP Sec. 6821; 8 CP Sec. 2689.)

A member cannot move to postpone the motion for the previous question. In Jefferson's language, "it would be absurd to postpone the previous question . . . and thus separate the appendage from its principle. . . ." (Jefferson's Manual, House Rules Sec. 451.)

—15—

AMENDMENTS

Sec. 112. Kinds of Amendments

Amending a proposition can raise complex and difficult parliamentary problems, if only because of the seemingly confusing terminology involved. In addition to simple amendments, known as amendments "to the text," there are amendments to amendments, substitute amendments, amendments to substitute amendments, and amendments in the nature of a substitute. (See Rule XIX, House Rules.)

An amendment in the nature of a substitute and a substitute amendment are not the same thing. (8 Cannon's Precedents[1] Sec. 2883.) A substitute amendment offers new language to replace the language contained in a pending amendment to the text. An amendment in the nature of a substitute offers all new language for the entire pending proposition.

In some organizations amendments are offered after a proposition has been read in full. In others the proposition, after general debate, is read for amendment under a five-minute rule and on a section-by-section basis. Amendments to a section are in order after it has been read, and before the secretary begins to read the next section. (8 CP Secs. 2354, 2866.) However, at the conclusion of the reading of a proposition for amendment, an amendment in the nature of a substitute for the original proposition may again be offered.

Committee amendments should be considered before amendments from the floor are in order. (8 CP Secs. 2862, 2863.)

The five-minute rule permits pro forma amendments, such as "I move to strike the last word," by which device a member may gain the floor for five minutes to discuss a pending amendment. (5 Hinds' Precedents[2] Sec. 5778; 8 CP Sec. 2591.)

[1] Hereinafter cited as CP.
[2] Hereinafter cited as HP.

201

A point of order against an amendment must be raised before debate on the amendment has begun (8 CP Sec. 6891); otherwise it will be overruled as coming too late, even though valid. The purpose of this rule is to save the time of the assembly in debating a proposition that might be ruled out on a point of order.

"The natural order in considering and amending any paper is," according to Jefferson, "to begin at the beginning, and proceed through it by paragraphs. . . ." And Jefferson recognized the general rule that "when a latter part has been amended, you cannot recur back and make any alteration in a former part." (Jefferson's Manual, House Rules Sec. 413.)

If an amendment covers more than one section, the amendment must be offered to the first section to be amended, even if it is only a technical change at that point and not the place where the real substance of the amendment is to be found. However, this cumbersome process can be avoided by the offering member obtaining unanimous consent to offer the entire amendment en bloc when the first affected section is under consideration.

Amendments are not in order while a point of order is pending. And amendments that have been disposed of cannot be offered again in the same form. For example, an amendment identical to one previously disagreed to is not in order. (2 HP Secs. 1328-36.)

Some motions are not amendable. A simple motion to adjourn is not subject to amendment, nor is the motion to lay on the table or for the previous question. A motion to postpone indefinitely is also impervious to amendment. (See 5 HP Sec. 5754.)

Jefferson set forth the rule that where amendment and postponement compete, postponement is first put, the reason being that the question of amendment is not suppressed by postponing the main question, but remains before the organization whenever the main question is resumed. (Jefferson's Manual, House Rules Sec. 449 Clause 4, Rule XVI.)

Sec. 113. Permissible Pending Amendments; Disposition

When a proposition is open to amendment there may be pending: (1) an amendment to the text; (2) an amendment to that amendment; (3) a substitute amendment for the original amendment; and (4) an amendment to the substitute amendment. (See Rule XIX, House Rules.) These four amendments (and only these) may be pending at one time. But as each is disposed of, another of the same class may be offered. (See 5 HP Sec. 5753; 8 CP Sec. 2883.)

Amendments beyond those listed above are considered to be amendments in the third degree and may not be offered. (See 5 HP Sec. 5754; 8 CP Sec. 2888.) Jefferson put the matter succinctly: "If an amendment be moved to an amendment, it is admitted; but it would not be admitted in another degree, to wit, to amend an amendment to an amendment of a main question. This would lead to too much embarrassment. The line must be drawn somewhere, and usage has drawn it after the amendment to the amendment." (Jefferson's Manual, House Rules, Sec. 454.)

Offered amendments must be disposed of in the following order. (See House Rules Sec. 823.)

> 1.   Amendments to the original amendment to the text are disposed of first. Only one may be pending against the amendment to the text at a time, but as quickly as it is disposed of, another may be offered.
>
> 2.   Amendments to the substitute amendment to the text are voted on next.
>
> 3.   The perfected substitute amendment to the text is then voted on.
>
> 4.   The perfected amendment to the text is voted on last, even though a substitute for the original amendment has been agreed to.

Sec. 114. Germaneness Requirements

Amendments are not in order unless germane to the question or proposal that is pending. (See Rule XVI Clause 7, House Rules.) For example, a motion that the organization purchase a computer is not subject to an amendment that would provide for the purchase of a warehouse. The correct procedure is to dispose of the original or main motion by vote, and then move on to a consideration of the next proposition.

The rule of germaneness, which is fundamental to any sound parliamentary system, means simply that the proposed amendment must not be on a subject different from that under consideration. (5 HP Sec. 5825.) The rule applies to amendments reported by committees as well as to amendments offered from the floor. (5 HP Sec. 5806.) The fundamental purpose of an amendment must be germane to the fundamental purpose of the main proposition. (8 CP Sec. 2911.)

When an amendment is offered to an amendment, the former must be germane to the latter as well as to the main proposition. (8

CP Sec. 2924.) However, an amendment simply striking out words from the main proposal is usually, though not necessarily, germane. (5 HP Sec. 5805; 8 CP Sec. 2918.)

Certain tests have been established in determining whether or not an amendment is germane. They are as follows:

1.   One individual proposition may not be amended by another individual proposition, even though the two belong to the same class. (8 CP Secs. 2963-66.) Thus, to a provision relating to a clerk of one committee, an amendment pertaining to a clerk on another committee is not germane. (5 HP Sec. 5833.) Likewise, to a proposition pertaining to cotton futures, an amendment adding wheat, corn, and other agricultural products is not germane. (8 CP Sec. 3001.)

2.   A specific subject may not be amended by a provision general in nature, even when of the class of the specific subject. (5 HP Secs. 5843-46; 8 CP Secs. 2997, 2998.) For example, to a proposition pertaining to corporations engaged in interstate commerce, an amendment relating to all corporations is not germane. (5 HP Sec. 5842.)

3.   A general subject may be amended by specific propositions of the same class. (8 CP Secs. 3002, 3009, 3012.) For example, to a proposition providing for the construction of buildings in two cities, an amendment providing for similar buildings in several other cities is germane. (5 HP Sec. 5840.)

4.   Two subjects are not necessarily germane because they are related. For example, to a proposition pertaining to the terms of certain elected officials, an amendment changing the manner of their election is not germane. (5 HP Sec. 5882.)

—16—

DEBATE

Sec. 115. Opening Debate; Recognizing Members

Under parliamentary law, the presiding officer has broad discretionary powers in recognizing members. It has been the rule since Jefferson's time that if two or more members rise to speak, the presiding officer determines who was the first to rise, and so recognizes him, unless the recognized member voluntarily gives way to the other. (Jefferson's Manual, House Rules Sec. 356.) There is ordinarily no appeal from the decision of the presiding officer in this respect. (8 Cannon's Precedents[1] Secs. 2429, 2646, 2762.)

Recognition is obtained by a member by waiting until the previous speaker has concluded his remarks, and then rising and addressing the presiding officer, who recognizes him by name, or as "The gentleman from. . . ." (Jefferson's Manual, House Rules Sec. 354; model rules on debate, see Sec. 44 *supra*.)

Although the presiding officer has much discretionary power in recognizing members, there are certain procedures that he should follow in this respect. For example, he should recognize a member who rises to make a motion to table before the member entitled to prior recognition for debate has begun his remarks. (5 Hinds' Precedents[2] Secs. 5391-95; 8 CP Secs. 2649, 2650.) Similarly, a member rising to refer a matter to a committee is entitled to prior recognition; and when the order of business brings before the assembly a certain matter from a committee, the presiding officer should first recognize, for motions as to its disposition, the member who represents the committee that has reported it. (2 HP Sec. 1447; 6 CP Secs. 306, 514.) For these reasons, it is especially helpful to the presiding officer to have a parliamentarian at his side during periods when debate or other floor procedures are anticipated.

The presiding officer, in exercising his discretion, should fol-

[1] Hereinafter cited as CP.

[2] Hereinafter cited as HP.

low certain general priorities in recognizing members. These priorities are not inflexible, but should be followed in the absence of a controlling bylaw. These priorities are as follows: The member who offers a proposal should have the first opportunity to be heard. The member who is opposed to the proposition should be given an opportunity to follow the member who is in favor thereof. A member who has not engaged in a discussion should be recognized ahead of one who has already spoken. And a member who rarely speaks should be recognized ahead of the member who is constantly on his feet.

The presiding officer may refuse to recognize any person whose name is not on the clerk's roll. (1 HP Sec. 86.) And he has the right to refuse to recognize or give the floor to anyone whose sole purpose is to obstruct the transaction of business.

Sec. 116. Right to the Floor; Interruptions

It was Jefferson's view that when a member stands up to speak, "no question is to be put, but he is to be heard unless the House overrule him." (Jefferson's Manual, House Rules, Sec. 355.) It is still the rule today that in the House no question is put as to the right of a member to the floor, although there is a procedure for calling him to order and dealing with him for any infraction of the rules. (See Rule XIV Clause 4, House Rules.)

It is a fundamental principle of parliamentary law that every member of an organization has a right to a voice in determining its affairs at its business meetings. The right of a member to speak must include, as well, the right to be heard. If the conversation of other members in the background interferes with this right, he may ask the presiding officer to intervene and to put a stop to it. Indeed, it is the duty of the presiding officer to maintain order at all times during debate. He should not permit a member to speak without first addressing the chair, nor permit the members to talk back and forth in such a way as to disrupt the meeting.

Nevertheless, in the words of Thomas Jefferson, "If a member finds that it is not the inclination of the House to hear him, and that by conversation or any other noise they endeavor to drown his voice, it is his most prudent way to submit to the pleasure of the House, and sit down. . . ." (See House Rules Sec. 365.) Of course, in the House of Representatives, where the motion for the previous question and various time limitations upon debate are available, it has been generally unnecessary to resort to Jefferson's method of suppressing a tedious member. (5 HP Sec. 5445.)

When a member wishes to interrupt someone who has the floor, he must first address the presiding officer and obtain recognition. (6 CP Sec. 193.) In fact, when a member has been recognized by the presiding officer and given the floor for a specified period of time, he may not ordinarily be interrupted by another member during that period without his consent even for the purpose of propounding a parliamentary inquiry. In other words, once he obtains recognition, he has the right to the floor. The right to speak is, however, subject to the following rules:

> 1. The member's remarks must pertain to the question being debated; if he digresses, the presiding officer may interrupt him to insist that he confine his remarks to the pending question.
> 2. The member's remarks must be kept free of personal references; the motion being considered is the subject of the debate, not the member who proposed it.
> 3. The member's remarks must avoid personal invective. Offensive language is sufficient cause for the presiding officer to suspend the member's continued right to speak. (5 HP Sec. 5161.)
> 4. A member's right to speak, either for or against a particular motion, is always subject to interruption by a point of order that he is not proceeding in order or is using offensive language. (2 HP Sec. 1247.)
> 5. A member's right to speak is always subject to any time limitations that have been imposed on the debate.

Sec. 117. Controlling Time for Debate

Orderly debate requires a watchful eye and a skillful approach. It requires much advance planning by all concerned. Time should be carefully allotted in advance and according to the subject matter and its importance as related to other items of business. Those who are to speak for or against a particular proposal should be identified ahead of time, and arrangements should be made for the allotment of time to each. If a particular subject is to be given over to informal discussion among the members at large, they should be notified in advance of the amount of time available for this purpose.

Debate in the House of Representatives and in many other membership organizations is subject to three general time limitations. They are: (1) the hour rule for general debate; (2) the special "rule" or resolution that specifies and controls the amount of time to be devoted to debate in certain proceedings; and (3) the five-minute rule, which applies to debate on amendments. (See Model Rule XII, Sec. 44 *supra*.)

The Hour Rule

The hour rule in the House prevents a member from speaking more than one hour except as otherwise specifically provided. (Rule XIV Clause 2, House Rules.) A member who has been recognized under the hour rule controls the floor during that period. He may yield part or parts or all of his time to one or more other members, as he pleases, for questions; but if he yields to another member for the purpose of offering an amendment or a motion, or making a statement, he loses the floor. (5 HP Secs. 5021, 5030, 5031; 8 CP Sec. 2476.)

The hour rule applies to debate on a question of privilege (5 HP Sec. 4990), as well as to special orders to speak on any subject at the end of the day after the legislative business of that day has been completed.

The Special Rule

Of course, the membership may agree to any amount of time —from one or two minutes to several hours—pursuant to a unanimous-consent request. In practice, the House in adopting a "special rule" for the consideration of a bill sets the amount of time to be allocated in debate, depending on the nature and complexity of the measure. Such special rules may also provide that the time is to be divided and controlled equally—usually between the chairman and the ranking minority member of the committee that reported the measure.

The Five-minute Rule

In most membership organizations the five-minute rule is used to govern debate on amendments. Debate on amendments may also be changed or limited in various ways by the terms of the "special rule" under which the membership is operating.

The five-minute rule applies to pro forma (see Sec. 112 *supra*) as well as substantive amendments. (House Rules Sec. 870.)

On a motion to recommit with instructions, after the previous question has been ordered "it always shall be in order to debate such motion for ten minutes before the vote is taken on that motion, one half of such time to be given to debate by the mover of the motion and one half to debate in opposition to the motion." (Rule XVI Clause 4, House Rules.)

There are many situations in which no debate is permitted. Primarily, these are:

1. On motions to adjourn, to lay on the table, or for the previous question. (Rule XVI Clause 4, House Rules.)

2. On a motion to fix the day to which the assembly shall adjourn. (5 HP Sec. 5380; 8 CP Sec. 2648.)

3. On appeals from the decision of the presiding officer on the priority of business or on irrelevancy of debate. (5 HP Secs. 5056-63.)

4. Motions for change of reference to committees. (7 CP Sec. 2126.)

5. On the appeal in the case of a member called to order for transgressing the rules. (Rule XIV Clause 4, House Rules; 5 HP Secs. 5161-63.)

6. Questions relating to the priority of business, although debate on a point of order is within the discretion of the presiding officer since it is for his information in deciding the matter. (8 CP Secs. 3440-48.)

The One-minute Rule

It is the practice in many membership organizations for the presiding officer to recognize individual members by unanimous consent for no more than one minute during a brief period following the reading of the minutes, at the beginning of each day's session. The member so recognized may deliver a brief statement on any topic, make an announcement, request information from the chair, or make a request for a special order (usually, permission to speak at length after the membership has finished its business). The member may deliver his remarks orally, read them in part and submit the remainder, or submit a written statement.[3]

[3]See, for this informal practice, *Congressional Record*, 75th Cong., 1st sess., pp. 3645, 5373; 79th Cong., 1st sess., p. 839.

—17—

VOTING

Sec. 118. Right to Vote

The voting rights of members should be, and ordinarily are, spelled out in specific terms in the bylaws as well as the organization's standing rules. (See Model Rules, Sec. 44 *supra*.) In many states the identification of voting rights of members is a statutory requirement. However, even where the applicable statutes are silent on the subject, it is of the utmost importance that the organization's constitution and bylaws spell out such voting rights. It is not sufficient that they be recognized merely in the articles of incorporation; this is so because very few organizations furnish their members with copies of the articles of incorporation, whereas most see to it that their members get copies of the bylaws. And if the bylaws are silent on the subject, members will find themselves without an authoritative source of information concerning their voting rights.

The voting rights of members may be categorized as either one-member-one-vote voting or as proportional voting. The one-member-one-vote method of voting is the most commonly used voting system employed by membership organizations, including legislative bodies. Illustrative of a rule or bylaw that adopts the one-member-one-vote concept is set out below.

> Every member in good standing shall be entitled to one (1) vote and only one (1) vote in all meetings of the membership.

Voting according to the number of shares held by a member is permitted in those membership organizations that issue stock. In such organizations each member has at least one vote, since each member must have at least one share of capital stock in the organization. The more stock owned, the greater the voting power. Typical of a bylaw provision that makes use of this voting system is as follows:

> In all proceedings, each shareholder shall be entitled to vote one (1) vote for each share of stock held by him.

An unhealthy situation arises where disproportionate voting power is acquired by one man or a relatively small group. To encourage widespread participation among members and to avoid centralization of power in relatively small groups of members, it is desirable that the bylaws incorporate the one-man-one-vote concept described above.

However, proportional voting is appropriate in large federated organizations in which the membership consists in whole or in part of a number of smaller individual associations. In such instances, the largest individual member-association has the greatest vote in determining the affairs of the parent body. Typical of the bylaws that make use of this voting method is set out below.

> Each member-association shall have one (1) vote and shall have one (1) additional vote for each full one hundred (100) of its own individual members or majority fraction thereof (fifty-one [51] or more).

Delegate Voting Systems

Just as an organization may use the delegate system in voting for members of the board of directors, so may it use the delegate system in voting on issues brought before the membership. This method is used particularly by organizations with memberships spread over a wide area. Under this procedure, the ballot of one delegate may represent the vote of ten or fifty or more individual members. Such a voting procedure does not depart from the concept of one-man-one-vote. Each delegate may cast as many votes at any meeting as the members of the group represented by him could cast if present at that meeting.

Sec. 119. Majorities, Pluralities, and Ties

It is axiomatic that the majority rules in any democratic institution, and membership organizations are no exception to this doctrine. "The voice of the majority decides," wrote Jefferson, "for the *lex majoris partis* is the law of all councils, elections, &c., where not otherwise expressly provided." (House Rules Sec. 508.)

However, there are differing rules as to what constitutes a majority. The "majority" is sometimes defined as being "any number greater than one half," in which case any number in excess of 50 percent is a simple majority. But the question still remaining is, "Fifty percent of what?" All of the members? A quorum? The total votes cast? All of the members present?

To avoid such confusion, the bylaws should define the word "majority" as applied to votes by the membership. In the absence of a specific definition in the bylaws, however, any number over 50 percent of the members of an organization constitutes a quorum, and one over 50 percent of a quorum (or 25 percent of the membership) constitutes the "majority" whenever a majority vote is required.

For certain important decisions, such as changing the structure of the organization or amending the bylaws, many organizations in their bylaws require a vote that is larger than a simple majority, sometimes two thirds, or even as much as 70 percent of a quorum. Such rules are intended to ensure widespread support on fundamental issues. But they also, of course, make it possible for the minority to thwart the will of the majority. Thus, in an organization consisting of 300 members, a proposition requiring a two-thirds vote can be defeated by as few as 101 members.

A "plurality" is a kind of vote that occurs when there are more than two alternatives, or more than two candidates to be chosen from. An issue or candidate is said to have a "plurality" when the issue or candidate receives an excess of the votes cast over those cast for any other, though still not a majority of all the votes cast. In other words, it is possible to have a plurality but not a majority vote for one of the issues or candidates. (1 HP Secs. 221, 222.) A plurality is a total of votes greater than any one of the others received, but not greater than the combined votes received by all the others. Unless the rules or bylaws specifically permit it, a plurality is not sufficient to carry a motion or elect a candidate.

Tie votes are relatively common, especially in organizations with a small membership. In the case of a tie vote, the presiding officer may cast the deciding vote, unless he has already voted. That is, he may vote to make or break a tie. If, after he has voted, the vote is a tie, the proposal falls under the general rule that a majority is "the number greater than one half." (See also Rule I Clause 6, House Rules.)

Sec. 120. Proxy Voting

A proxy vote is a vote whereby one person is substituted for, or deputized by, another to represent him and vote for him at a meeting. (Proxy voting in committees of the House, see Rule XI Clause 27, House Rules.) Proxy voting is on the decline in the United States. And although members of the House of Lords in England have the privilege of voting by proxy, the system is in abeyance even there.

No one has the inherent right to vote by proxy unless it is legally provided for in the bylaws. In this regard, some state statutes under which membership organizations are incorporated prohibit proxy voting. Others permit it. But unless a specific provision is written into the bylaws authorizing proxy voting, an organization is prohibited from using this method.

One way of furthering widespread participation of members is to require that a member must be present personally in order to vote. This requirement is found in many state statutes that apply to membership organizations. However liberal the statutes may be, the bylaws should permit proxy voting only where absolutely necessary.

Proxy voting is in disfavor because of the recognition that persons not in attendance do not hear the debate and are not as well informed on the issues as those present. Proxy voting is also discouraged because of the danger that someone might gain enough proxies to control the annual meeting and outvote the members in attendance and voting in person. For these reasons, proxy voting should be permitted only where geographical considerations require it; and then the bylaws should provide for a limitation on the number of proxies that any one person is permitted to vote and require that the matter to be voted on be specified.

A bylaw that prohibits proxy voting is set out below.

> Each member shall be entitled to one (1), and only one (1), vote. There shall be no proxy voting.

A bylaw that permits proxy voting, but places a limit on its use, is set out below.

> Every member shall have one (1) vote. Voting by proxy shall be allowed, but a member shall be permitted to vote only one (1) such proxy, which shall be in writing and which shall specify the matter to which the proxy shall apply.

Sec. 121. Taking the Vote

There are many ways in which a vote may be taken, the most common being the so-called *viva voce* vote. In taking a voice vote, the presiding officer calls first for the affirmative vote, "All those in favor of this motion say 'Yea' or 'Aye,' " and then calls for the negative, "All those opposed say 'Nay' or 'No.' " The presiding officer then determines, on the basis of the relative volume, whether or not a proposal or motion has carried. (Rule I Clause 5, House Rules.)

In the event that the relative volume of voices voting is uncertain, the presiding officer may call for a show of hands or for a rising vote. He does so by asking, "Will those in favor of the motion please rise." After counting, he then requests, "Will those opposed to the motion please rise." He then announces the result.

Still another method of voting is the roll call, or yea and nay, vote. In this kind of vote, the secretary calls the roll and records the yes or no vote of each member as he responds. (Rule XV Clause 1, House Rules.)

In many organizations the membership may wish to vote pursuant to a policy that does not require each member to disclose his vote. This may be done by ballot.

The present methods of voting are summarized as follows:

1.   *Voice vote.* This method is the least time-consuming, with members calling out "Aye" and "No." It should not be used where the vote is close.

2.   *Division vote.* In a division vote members voting in the affirmative stand until counted and then members voting in the negative stand until counted, a procedure that takes more time, of course. It is a more accurate method of determining the number of votes on a question, but may not allow time for absent members to attend and does not provide a record of each member's vote. (House Rules Sec. 630.)

3.   *Teller vote.* In a teller vote, tellers are appointed by the presiding officer and take places at given checkpoints; the presiding officer then directs the members voting in the affirmative to pass between the tellers and be counted. He then directs those members voting in the negative to pass between the tellers. (House Rules Sec. 630.)

4.   *Ballots.* Under this method, a member writes the name of the candidate of his choice on a card if voting in the affirmative or on a different card if voting in the negative. Then members voting drop the cards into ballot boxes, with ballots then being counted by tellers. (Rule XXXVIII House Rules.)

5.   *Roll call.* Under this method, a clerk calls the roll of members, and they respond as their names are called. This method provides a record of how each member voted.

On a voice vote any member may demand a division, or the presiding officer may call for a division without suggestion from the floor. (5 Hinds' Precedents[1] Sec. 5926.)

A demand for tellers should be supported by a specified number of members (Rule I Clause 5, House Rules) but may be ordered by the presiding officer on his own initiative if he is in doubt. (5 HP Sec. 5985.)

The presiding officer is not required to vote unless his vote would be decisive either to make or break a tie. (Rule I Clause 6, House Rules.) His name is not called unless on his request and then at the end of the roll.

Sec. 122. Vote Announcements; Recapitulations

The presiding officer should announce the result of the vote as soon as voting is completed. If it has been a voice vote, he should say, "In the opinion of the chair, the ayes [*or noes*] have it. The motion is carried [*or lost*]." In taking a vote, the presiding officer should put the question on the affirmative first; and then on the negative. The same sequence is followed in announcing the result.

Once the vote is begun and members are responding on any motion or proposal, no further debate shall be in order until the voting is finished and the votes counted. A member must await the announcement of the result of the vote before he may move to reconsider.

Where a member questions a voice vote as announced by the presiding officer, he may call for a division of the assembly, which will require an actual count of the affirmative and negative votes by the chair. Where a vote has been taken by ballot or by roll call, the presiding officer should announce the number of votes, saying, "On this question the vote is: 210 for, 205 against. The motion is carried."

Where the rules do not provide for a procedure for disclosing how an absent colleague would vote, if he were present, such procedure is permitted by unanimous consent only. (6 Cannon's Precedents[2] Sec. 200.)

A member may change his vote at any time before the vote is finally and conclusively announced. Thereafter, he will not be rec-

---

[1] Hereinafter cited as HP.

[2] Hereinafter cited as CP.

ognized to change his vote. (See 5 HP Secs. 5931-33 and 8 CP Secs. 3070, 3123, 3124.)

In the U.S. House of Representatives the presiding officer has discretionary power in the ordering of vote recapitulations, although, as a general rule, he will not order a recapitulation if the difference between the majority and minority votes is greater than four votes.[3] The presiding officer may order the vote recapitulated either before the announcement of the result or after such announcement. (5 HP Secs. 6049, 6064; 8 CP Secs. 3125, 3128.) However, a member may not change his vote on recapitulation if the result has been announced. (8 CP Sec. 3124.)

Where the presiding officer through an error announces a result different from that actually had, his subsequent announcement of the changed result is authoritative. To effectuate such a change, he may entertain a motion for correcting the minutes with the vote as finally ascertained. (8 CP Sec. 3162.) In this regard, the presiding officer, having voted to make or break a tie, may not again vote, but he may exercise his right to withdraw his vote in case a correction shows it to have been unnecessary. (5 HP Sec. 5971.)

[3] 87 Congressional Record 6897, 77th Cong. 1st sess., Aug. 7, 1941.

—18—

ADJOURNMENT

Sec. 123. Timing; Form

Motions to adjourn fall into three categories: (1) the simple motion to adjourn, (2) the motion to adjourn to a time certain, and (3) the motion to fix the time to adjourn to a time certain.

A membership organization may adjourn a meeting at any time, and this is true even during its period of organization and before the election of a presiding officer. (1 Hinds' Precedents[1] Sec. 89.) The motion to adjourn enjoys the highest precedence and privilege, and even other questions of privilege must yield to it. (3 HP Sec. 2521.) Indeed, a majority of the members may vote to adjourn even though a quorum is not present. (8 Cannon's Precedents[2] Sec. 2642.)

In the U.S. House of Representatives the rules permit (1) the motion to adjourn and (2) the motion to adjourn to a day and time certain. (Rule XVI Clause 4, House Rules.) Thus, when the hour of daily meeting is not fixed, a motion to adjourn with appropriate language may be used to fix it. (5 HP Secs. 5362, 5363.)

The motion to adjourn may be made even though the presiding officer is absent, as where the clerk is presiding. (1 HP Sec. 228.) The motion may be made after a vote has been ordered but before the roll call has begun. (5 HP Sec. 5366.) However, the motion should not be permitted to interrupt the act of voting on another motion. (5 HP Sec. 5360.) And when no question is under debate, the simple motion to adjourn should not displace the motion to fix the day to which the organization shall adjourn. (5 HP Sec. 5381.)

The simple motion to adjourn is neither debatable nor amendable, and carries by a majority vote. (5 HP Secs. 5359, 5360.) The motion must be put to a vote immediately after it has been made.

[1] Hereinafter cited as HP.

[2] Hereinafter cited as CP.

Neither another motion nor an appeal may intervene before the taking of the vote. (5 HP Sec. 5361.)

The motion to adjourn to a time certain or to fix the time to adjourn to a time certain is amendable but not debatable, and carries by a majority vote.

INDEX

Section numbers are indicated in (**boldface**)

TABLE OF MOTIONS

(For discussion see Secs. 44, 106–114, and 123)

	Debate	Amendment	Vote
The Main Motion[1]	Yes	Yes	Majority
Dispositive Motions[2]			
(In order of rank)			
Question of Consideration[3]	No	No	Majority
To Lay on the Table[4]	No	No	Majority
For the Previous Question[5]	No	No	Majority
To Postpone to a Day Certain[6]	Yes	Yes	Majority
To Refer to Committee[6]	Yes[7]	Yes[7]	Majority
To Amend	Yes	Yes	Majority
To Postpone Indefinitely[6]	Yes	No	Majority
To Close or Limit Debate	No	Yes[8]	Majority
Procedural Motions			
(In order of rank)			
Point of Order[9]	Yes[10]	No	No vote
To Appeal a Ruling	Yes	No	Majority
Parliamentary Inquiry	No	No	No vote
To Reconsider a Vote	Yes[11]	No	Majority
To Suspend the Rules	Yes	No	Two-thirds
To Discharge a Committee (from consideration of a proposition)	Yes	No	Majority
Motions to Adjourn[12]			
(In order of rank)			
To Adjourn	No	No	Majority
To Adjourn to a Time Certain	No	Yes	Majority
To Fix the Time to Adjourn to a Time Certain	No	Yes	Majority
To Recess[13]	No	Yes	Majority